ASTRAL JOURNEYS

FROM

THE EDGE

by

Sergio Parada

ISBN: 978-1-387-76140-1

Lulu Publishing

<u>Introduction</u>

I began astral projecting when I was 17 - I am now 47. In my hundreds of experiences I am convinced now more than ever that the astral is the next step in human evolution. Just the idea that we have the inborn ability to travel to other worlds is exciting enough, but the astral is also a place of great beauty and mystery, a source of incredible knowledge, and a place where we can meet other astral travelers.

In this book, I've chronicled some of my numerous astral excursions. When I initially began having these encounters, I had very little knowledge. So, at this early point in my research, I decided to become my own scientist and go it alone. I would examine this new world which I was leaping into with a scientific eye and come to my own conclusions.

Here are my some of my experiences in the astral...

Alpha Pine

July 9, 2019

Last night, I had an interesting astral projection (AP). I went to sleep and programmed myself for an exit. After about 15 minutes I felt my astral body unhook from my physical and I slowly exited. I emerged down a long tunnel.

People were walking down the tunnel. I was conscious and felt as though something stunning lay ahead of me on this route. I got on the conveyor belt and let it take me down the tunnel. I remember seeing a father with his two small children and they were holding hands. Lots of people were there all going in the same direction. Then I came to a black mist. People were going in and disappearing. Finally, it was my turn and I went into darkness.

The next sensation was movement. I was being hurled at a breakneck speed. And I didn't have a body anymore. A tiny light appeared in the distance and gradually grew until it became enormous before me. Little lights were going toward it, being absorbed, but my way veered away from it just as the big star vanished.

The next thing I knew, I had a body again and was standing on solid ground. The first thing I noticed was an English sign that read, "Welcome to Alpha Pine." It looked like a shopping mall. I went on a walkabout, and I discovered stores and even fast food restaurants. I was intrigued about what astral fast food was like, so I entered this fast-food restaurant with a hamburger sign and an odd name. There were a few people in the restaurant when I went in, but there was no line to stand in to get food. I inquired about obtaining food with a coworker. He escorted me to this machine, which pushed a button, and out came a hamburger wrapped in paper. I thanked him and departed the doors that led outside.

Outside, I saw snow-capped mountains and a plethora of pine trees. The air was fresh, and I could hear ravens cawing to one another. Some flying creatures caught my attention. Well, at this point I really wanted to try my hamburger so I unwrapped it and took a bite. It tasted like a hamburger and it was yummy but the texture was different. Not like normal bun but fluffier like it was half made of air.

I kept walking and made it to the entrance of the mall... it said Alpha Pine Mall.

Get to Heaven

July 13, 2019

This time after exiting from my body I went out my side wall and I went straight UP as far and as long as I could! I wanted to get to Heaven. To really see the LIGHT! I turned on my hand jets and just kept on going and going straight up and up and up. My hand jets are a practice I developed where I could push off by pushing force out of my hands. It's a very handy technique to master as it lets you repulse things and people with our hands in the astral.

I went up and up and through so many layers and worlds full of strange beings and lands. It was amazing to see how much different stuff is out there. And how absolutely HUGE this universe is.

There was this pretty place with spheres of metal that floated and resonated. I sat there on a deserted hill and watched them go by - taking a breather. Then I remember I landed inside a tunnel. It was full of children hurrying around and in fear. I rested at another place full of fog. Hills were everywhere with abandoned ruins and strange writing on the rocks.

On my way up I also remember passing huge galaxies and nebulas. They were a little dark... not like regular galaxies we view with a telescope. I heard a voice tell me that the reason they were half dimmed was because I was viewing them from a great height. All the suns put together would look like a dark blemish as viewed from Heaven.

As I went up I encountered a flow that went opposite me - downward. The Negative Power. I pushed so hard against it. Every time I weakened it was there waiting to pull me back down to the trenches from where I had come.

There where many types of powerful astral beings who played tricks on me and tested me. I mean big GIANT astral entities. One of them took my shoes! The tests were over in a matter of seconds because I was so adamant in reaching the Light. One test... they fondled me with a beautiful naked child. I heard a big deep voice say "Let's see how he reacts to flesh." I just kept on saying "LIGHT!" and I kept going higher and higher.

At one point I finally had a taste of the Light. It was so beautiful. I deep tunnel opened in front of me and it was pure Light. But it was gone so soon. I had to engage my hand jets on overdrive to just keep going.

I went to sleep at 12 am, projected immediately, and got back at 2 am. I was out there for 2 hours!

<u>Observations #1</u>

July 15, 2019

When I first started astral projecting I was surprised at the amount of darkness or outright black in the astral. Indeed, I think as physical beings we live on a plane where the Light doesn't shine all that brightly. Sometimes when I exit my body, I'll go outside around 4 am and it is literally pitch black. I can see this would be a turn off for someone beginning to AP. It sure was to me. And there are shadow beings floating in that darkness sometimes. I have found they are harmless however... usually.

But as my practice progressed I had fewer and fewer "black night" experiences. I still get them though where my street is so dark and lonely it's very scary. Now, sometimes, the lights will be on in some of the houses. Or there are humans dancing the streets or instead of pitch black it's morning come or early twilight with the sky in all pretty colors.

So for me, right now, my goal is to increase my Light level. Being a physical being bordering dark astral planes I think in this I will not be completely successful but I'd like to see more Light in my projections.

I think a lot of people think astral projecting means gardens of light and heaven-like environments (and they are out there) but I think we are also meant to experience the darkness and within that experience make choices as to who and what we want to become. I also think that we as humans, we are naturally protected by a guardian force that wishes us to seek the Light. But I also think the same guardian force wants to familiarize us with darkness as a teacher exposes his pupil to all subjects, not just the pretty ones. For me, the experience of the "Guardian" has been like a tourist guide, exposing me to all that is out there. How else can we grow?

This universe is made up of both the Light and the Darkness. There's so much out there... I think it's a mistake to expect that we will always end up in the Light. So like I said, I'm making my personal mission to strive for more Light and Love in my life and of course in my out of body experiences.

The Well

July 16, 2019

There are three modes of dreaming for me. There is dreaming asleep. That's usually what most dreams are for most people. There is dreaming lucidly. That's dreaming awake. And there is what I call dreaming the Dreamer, where you and your dreamer are not different but One. Last night I dreamed with my Dreamer.

When I'm lucid and I'm dreaming the Dreamer I am a different person. This person has confidence, he's super smart, very handsome, and very skillful. It's like lucidity but you are lucid as this new person with new memories and new skills. The dreamer in us is always our best selves. He is humorous, light sided, and always ready to do a good deed.

Well last night I was my Dreamer and I went down "the Well". It all started by me exiting my body and going through the wall. Outside was this girl dressed in a lavender dress with loose skirts. She was pretty and told me to get in the jeep which was parked next to my house and was red and white. She said that we were going to the Well so I could learn it. She also said she was sent by the Collaborators. This is a group of entities that have helped me before. The first time I met them they did an amazing healing on me.

We started driving and soon we were out of my neighborhood and into a dense forest road. The trees looked purple and blue and it was on the dark side. We came upon a large stone building and got out of the jeep by a gate that went out back. I followed my friend behind the small castle looking building toward a huge hole in the ground. There stood the Well. It was large with a diameter of perhaps 4 meters and looking down it looked deep with no water immediately discernible. That's when my friend did something to me and I became my Dreamer.

It's difficult to say what we did but me and this girl went down this Well and she showed me things. I was lucid in the astral not as a normal person but as this super me. I had access to all my astral knowledge and I used it to do mysterious things inside and down this well. Being back to my normal self I cannot recall exactly what we did but I remember a silence so quiet that it was deafening. Whatever this place was, it was not part of everyday life and it was special. From the intense quiet rose a song of silence yet I could hear it with my extended senses. It was audible but not with my ears but with my feeling. We went deeper and deeper down the Well. At this point I can't remember what else it was I discovered. I think those memories belong to my Dreamer only and are part of the other. The other part that I remember was visual like seeing a ring of fractals all around me.

Little Faeries

July 19, 2019

After I heard these little pip-squeak voices chatting to each other besides my bed I immediately astral projected to see what they were. On the floor was this little ping-pong ball of astral energy. When I approached it, it moved away. I quickly nabbed it in my hands from the floor and took a closer look.

The little voices were apparently coming from inside this ball. They were apparently upset. I could hear them talking to each other like they were in trouble. The ball in my hands was buzzing and vibrating. They sounded so Faery like little woodsen creatures. They were probably out to play. They just happened to be playing in my room!

I went outside and made a good distance between my house and put it on the grass. Immediately it started rolling away with little laughs and squeaks. I heard a few ridicules in my direction before it vanished from sight.

The Throwaway Kids

July 26, 2019

Last night I went to a not so good place. You could immediately tell it was a real place because the experience was so solidly lucid. I appeared on a vast plane like a flat desert. I saw some rude buildings up ahead. They weren't pretty, built strictly for function. Inside these buildings were rooms full of children. The place stank of human slobbery. The kids were wearing rags and packed into many small rooms. Most rooms had some kind of small television hung up on the wall.

I don't know who these kids were but there were tons. As I left the building I saw one adult walking toward me. She was just as dirty. She freaked me out so I wasn't going to talk to her. As she walked passed me she spoke and said, "Hello Death."

I guess she didn't see many of my kind here wherever kids are kept in slums like they've been thrown away. It also felt like my guiding force was showing me something of the "real world".

There are all kinds of places like that... I call them the badlands. Thankfully there are wonderful beautiful places which we can attain. It has to do with being a good person and showing your soul to God... so you can form a relationship with the Universe. Whatever that force is we're a part of it and we need to foster a relationship that will guarantee a good there after.

Elephant Park

July 29, 2019

I became lucid in the middle of a dream. Me and two regulars of my circle were being carted through a lush forest at night on three plush bean bags. They are just two friends I made in the astral and we go on adventures together. I don't really know them in real life but they seemed to be real people under the scrutiny of lucidity. So we hang out sometimes... I'll call them Bill and Ted.

We drifted through the dark forest to a lovely elephant park on bean bags! It was constructed of granite and featured ancient engravings. We got out of our seats to inspect the park. The elephants were kind, with a little one running around with us. So adorable. We returned to our cushions and continued our journey. We went to a monastery.

It was a white washed building made of stone and it was dark and quiet except in every room there are lots of candles on. But there was not a soul around.

We hiked down a path into town and there was a deathly still in the streets except for this huge cathedral where light was shining through. We entered and there was this huge dance going on with loud music. The music couldn't be heard until we opened the door.

I guess this is where I go into the dream because I remember really enjoying myself. Wish those memories were clearer but they fade in the light of day.

I was lucid again for one more moment. It was the inside of that large cathedral but dark now and full of beds. Everyone had gone to sleep. Me and my friends said goodbye and then we found our sleep.

Freedom!

August 2, 2019

I exited my body and since I fell asleep on my couch, I exited through the front door. The street was dark and I immediately looked to see which houses had their lights turned on. This means I can go in there and explore. But none of the houses looked like my neighborhood and as I walked down the street toward some lights I started seeing these huge heads above me. It was as if behind the houses there where lots of giraffes and their necks sorta made an arch over the street. But the giant giraffes over the street had the most alien and amazing faces. It was so real! I could see every detail of these animal things watching me walk down the street and I wondered what power it was that could be so artful.

Tonight was a breakthrough for me. I've finally figured out how to have total freedom. At one time, I became hungry, so I and a few others cooked dinner by merely thinking of different foods and pointing to a place on the table. It also tasted great, unlike my previous astral meals.

I got to watch the movies at this theater with a few people and we weren't just watching the movie we were creating it from our very own enhanced imaginations. They would add something and then I would add something and it appeared right on the screen. And things started reacting to each other until we were all laughing in our seats! Astral has some great tv.

I could fly and jump 100 feet at a time and the architecture of the buildings were so beautiful, whitewashed, and clean. Everyone I met was super friendly and in a happy mood. I was doing things I never have before, creating a world out of nothing and sharing the world that had already been created by others. It was a beautiful AP. This is what it's all about and I can't wait to see that world with those special astral eyes that makes everything so sharp and colorful.

To Fly!

August 9, 2019

After a few nights of restless sleep and foreboding dreams I finally had a joyous astral projection.

I looked around my room. It was quiet and homey. I quickly went out my wall and sprung into the air. I noticed that I was lighter than usual - almost as if something or someone was helping me float.

It was another beautiful night. The stars where out and they sparkled from above making the dark night gleam with a light all its own. I headed down the street floating on a cushion of air. I saw some people in their car driving my way and I heard their thoughts as the car passed under me.

"Look Mama, a flying boy!"

"That's amazing," commented the Father.

"That's one of God's children honey."

"Am I a God's children?"

The Mother laughed and said, "Of course you are darling. Someday we'll all get to fly like that."

I was a little startled. Everyone flies in their dreams... unless they don't know they are dreaming. The people in that car did not know they were asleep and in the astral. They were half-aware.

I headed north toward Canada. I picked up an incredible speed and traveled through valleys and neighborhoods full of green bushy trees and nestled little houses with their porch lights on. At one point I got tired and felt like landing.

I smoothly touched down on a stretch of road in some neighborhood in some city in some state. There where a few people there to greet me - a group of boys playing ball in the evening twilight.

"Wow! Where did you come from?" one of the boys asked. I felt like Superman just coming down from the sky.

"I'm from down south in Florida. Where am I now?" I asked.

"You're in Wisconsin!" one of the older boys said. Wisconsin? I sure had made the trip north alright!

They were very excited about my aerial acrobatics and wanted to try it themselves. They weren't very good at it though. They couldn't fly at all. Someone offered me a helmet and said I should use it in case I fell down out of the sky. I put on the helmet and it felt really good on my head.

They wanted to take me into their house. I knew they where dreaming and not in complete awareness but I played along. They took me into their building where they wanted me to "watch some TV with them". Oh oh! I quickly made my exit through a window which made them very mad. "Come back here you bastard!"

I continued flying north. I saw beautiful pastures, and lakes with little islands. There was an island full of beautiful girls in bikinis who made me want to stop. They were having a party with a bonfire and I could hear the music blasting.

Near shore's edge I spotted a lonesome girl. She was just standing there looking out unto the lake. I landed right next to her. She jumped in surprise. I smiled and she smiled back. I slowly put my arm around her shoulder and leaned in for a kiss. She leaned in as well and our lips touched. And then I woke up!

Circus

August 13, 2019

Last night I became lucid on a strange plane. There was some kind of regime going on this plane and there where soldiers walking the streets. Things looked organized but there were the start of dilapidated buildings and there was some refuse in the streets.

I saw a circus on one corner and a small mob was buying tickets trying to get in. The people were dressed in tacky worn clothes. I jumped the fence and went into the circus. I entered a tent where a few acrobats were practicing. I watched for awhile and then someone came over to me. It was one of the acrobats. He had a big mustache. "You shouldn't be here. You're in the wrong place. If you come with me I can get you out." He seemed earnest so I followed.

We went behind the tent into another tent that was dark and full of boxes. In one dark corner was a small tunnel in the corner. "Follow me," said the man and he got on all fours and went in. I followed. At the other end was a makeshift gang plank in mid air. All around was black but I could see that it was a bridge leading upward in thin wooden planks.

I finally made it to the other side and had to squeeze through this silky tunnel at the end. What met my eyes stunned me. It was a Garden of Eden of some sort. There were green hills that went on forever and small groves of trees dotted the land. The sun was out and the sky was that pure astral blue. The man had turned into some kind of minotaur but he looked badass with horns. The Minotaur said, "Stay here." And then he was gone, back into the tunnel.

Hold My Hand

August 26, 2019

I exited my body in one smooth motion by rolling out towards the left and then through the wall. Everything looked normal and it was a dark night. I headed towards my back yard. Instead of the fence that is usually there separating my neighbor's yard, there were lots of trees like a forest and a small dirt path leading into it.

My two cats were there too. I don't know if I was dreaming them or if they were also astral projecting. In the real world they were on my bed next to me asleep. They were playing and chasing each other. They started running down the path and so I followed.

The forest got deeper and deeper and then we made it to a clearing where the forest opened up. There was a nice bluish light surrounding everything so that instead of a scary dark forest, it felt homey and welcoming. There was a small pond there which was fed by a small gurgling river on the right. Toward the left was a hill where the land rose in a series of tiers. The tiers were connected by small stairs which where made of stone.

My two kitties disappeared and I looked around a little concerned. I spent awhile looking for them until in a lucid moment I realized and remembered I was projecting. I figured they were alright and went up some stairs to the third tier of the hill. There was a gazebo there with benches and I sat down and just relaxed for a while. My view wandered around my surroundings and I spied several people who were sitting on benches too above and below me.

Suddenly a group of girls came walking toward me. They were talking and very animated. One girl had short blond hair and was dressed in a nice little one piece with a very short skirt exposing her beautiful white legs. This was the girl that stopped and looked at me. "You have such nice hair," she said to me. "How do you get it to shine like that?" This came as a surprise to me so I just said what popped into my head. "I just wash it." She went on about my hair some more and then she took my hand. The other girls had gone and she sat down next to me and we held hands. I cuddled her hand and rubbed it a little and it felt really good.

I woke up a little after that and felt really happy. Sometimes all you need is for someone to hold your hand.

Starry Night

September 12, 2019

I haven't been APing lately... just a little here and there. But last night I decided to AP on purpose again. I got in my bean bag and got into my blanket and fell asleep. I watched myself falling asleep and I was tired so it was easy. At some point I fell asleep and went outside the front door. The first thing I saw were stars.

The sky was littered with some of the brightest stars I'd ever seen. The street was really dark but not black and the darkness felt thrilling. I looked down the street for any lights but there were none... except one. Far down the street was a lit bulb on a building like a church. I engaged my speeder-bike move and was there in a matter of seconds.

I was in front of the building and cars where going by in the street. I think I saw a jazzed up cop car. It was cool looking. I went into the building. At the desk was an old man with a little hat. I think he was like a security guard or something. Anyway, we introduced ourselves and went on to talk about APing and dreams. In the end I think I was talking to a fully conscious entity who understood me and had concepts pertaining to his own individualized experience. I just don't think he knew he was asleep. Maybe it was like two dreamers meeting... except I knew I was dreaming. Or maybe he was a phantom.. he obviously had some kind of life but I am stuck not knowing who these people are that populate my dreams and APs.

The Collaborator

September 18, 2019

I exited my body and slipped through my bedroom wall. I was outside and it was just dawning. Some of the neighborhood porch lights where still on so I picked the nearest house with a light and opened the door. Inside was a dark tunnel that went on a few meters toward an archway where I could see blue sky. I went down the tunnel and came out the other side.

I saw kids everywhere, mostly teenagers around sixteen years of age. Everyone was playing. Some were playing volleyball and soccer or rocking on swings or running or just in groups talking. It was a huge playground! Around the playground were two story houses in all colors. A group of young guys came toward me and we started talking.

Something was happening to my vision... it was hard to keep focused. "What's wrong?" said one of the boys. "It's my eyes, I can't see." The boy grabbed me by the bridge of the nose near my eyes and did something and suddenly I could see again. "Thanks, that's better," I said. "Come with us, there's a Collaborator in one of the houses. They'll take a look at you." I agreed and followed the leader to this pointy two story house.

We went into the house but there was a line to see the healer. I could feel myself waking up and I was antsy to see the healer because I knew I didn't have enough time to wait. Suddenly I was lifted into the air, floated up the stairs and into the "Collaborator's" room. There were many people inside. It was a pretty big room and it was carpeted with soft white carpet. I heard a voice say, "Ok now, everyone lay down on the floor. Now close your eyes and try to go to sleep."

I was gently dropped on a clear spot on the floor and I lay down. Around me I could see many young boys and girls doing the same. The lights dimmed and I closed my eyes and was still. The healing was about to begin.

I was a little afraid - like going to the doctor. Some really depressing things that are going on in my life right now came to the forefront of my mind. Before I knew it, I was crying like a baby. I was so sad. Then... then... I felt something crazy! Imagine being hit in the face with water from a hose on high. That's what it felt like. But it wasn't ordinary water. It was happy water because as I was drenched with this water I got so happy!

I started laughing out loud and the hose continued to water me all over my body. I laughed so hard! I was full of joy! And that's how I woke up... laughing my butt off in bed. It lasted the entire day. It felt like I was joyous and free all day and had this little glow in my heart.

Whatever that magic water was, it certainly did the trick. I don't think I've ever been that happy and laughed so hard. I wonder where that water comes from and who is in charge of dispersing it. It was a healing session after all.

Astral Storm

September 26, 2019

This AP scared me a little because it was on the intense side. It all started in a dream I was having. I felt a slight breeze tickle my face and I snapped into full lucidity! Snap!

I was with friends and they were all excited - a storm was coming, serious storm, an Awareness Storm. The information was percolating through my network of friends and we were all getting ready. We just wouldn't be lucid, we would be super lucid!

I don't exactly know how the information was spreading, but all my family and friends were congregating. We would take shelter at this building we all knew and usually take shelter in. I seemed to have access to a new vast knowledge about my astral life and could see how me and all my friends were connected to each other - a sort of astral network or community.

I found myself walking down a street with a group of my closest friends toward the building were we would take shelter. I was extra-lucidly aware of everything and had access to all my astral memories. The wind had picked up considerably and I could hear a low ominous moaning coming from the sky. It was dark and flashes of lighting were shooting down. Someone started screaming, "Run! Run! Run!"

We just made it to the building when the storm hit. Everyone found a room and hunkered down. The thing about an awareness storm is that it super-charges one's awareness. It can make someone extremely uncomfortable. Some see it as a chance to explore their awareness but there's always a chance of losing control and going crazy.

Outside the storm began screaming! As every screech came, my awareness would peak into a climax, and I had access to the deepest depths of my consciousness. I kneeled down in a corner and put my head between my knees. It was painful and totally disconcerting. Every time the storm would screech I kept getting more and more awareness. It was painful in that way. Too much awareness! Too much lucidity! Ahhhh!

Then someone was holding my hand. I looked up and it was my best-friend's sister. We hardly knew each other in real-life, but under the effects of the storm I could remember an ancient history together - lifetimes and lifetimes together. In many of them we had been married. Another storm screech went by and then she was in my arms and we held each other for dear life. Thanks to my super-charged awareness I could feel every part of her as we clung to one another. In essence we became one being.

The storm continued outside but we found relief in each other. Instead of the uncomfortable pain of too much consciousness we began looking forward to the storm surges. We would climax together and could feel infinity and eternity between us. It had absolutely nothing to do with sex. It felt like I had found my soul mate... someone who knew me and fit together with me perfectly. At this point any awareness of sex was obsolete. It was Love but love so pure and untainted by any carnal awareness. I have never felt anything like it in this current life. It was deep man... At one point we started conversing mind to mind and it was so blissful and intoxicating to share one mind.

I don't know how long we were lost in each other but the storm eventually blew off and me and all my friends "woke up".

Now, as I write this I realize that we are beings who live in two realities. One is our waking life but the other is our astral life and both are just as valid. It's in all our lucid experiences but also in all those we can't remember. We still have so much to discover about ourselves and this universe which we are a part of.

Plants with Briefcases

November 14, 2019

Last night I traveled to the farthest reaches of my known universe visiting alien worlds I never knew existed. It started like any normal AP. I flew around free as a bird looking for anything interesting. Well last night I found it. I came upon this laughing little girl. She seemed so strange and half there almost. I approached this being because it was new to my experience and wanted to find out what she or it was. Just a little laughing ghost girl dressed in strange Japanese tights it seemed. She just happened to be a scout from a galaxy far far away.

As soon as I touched her I was transported a million dimensions away. I ended up in a world inconceivable from mine. This world was perhaps millions of years ahead of us. They had astral technology and guided my astral body into a docking bay while I could hear a read-out of my body's abilities, "three raptures, two blades, and 309 maneuvers". What where they talking about?

I could see part of their astral technology as it held my astral body like a spider with millions of fibers of silk. It didn't seem so strange to me that other advanced civilizations would have astral airports and astral worlds on top of their physical worlds. I could see thousands of other souls coming into the airport, being grabbed by these silky pads, and being guided into the terminal. It was so beautiful. I wondered what kind of transformation a civilization must undergo to be able to grasp such concepts as astral technology. Not just that... a whole astral reality based on their physical reality with rules and laws of its own. Wow I thought.

I was set loose upon this alien world. When I asked one of the airport employees why I was being let go into their astral society he said, "Just part of professionalism." These guys had an open door policy for tourists.

I saw a lot of weird crap. I saw plants that walked around with little briefcases making errands in this large city. I saw strange looking people, some tall, some short, with all kinds of weird looks. Some looked like blue kitty-cats, some looked like pink koala bears. I passed a pet shop and saw a little girl (I think) playing with a bunch of tribble-like creatures. I held one and it purred in my hand. It was a wonderful sensation. I entered a park with huge fruit trees and asked a park employee if I could take a fruit from the tree. "Sure," he said, "it's just part of professionalism." I bit into it and it was the most tasty astral meal to date. I got to watch some of their television on some screens they had outside. It was AMAZING! I have never seen such eye-candy in my life. I just stared at it for the longest time. The commercials where the absolute best!

Anyway... I've never had an AP like this one. It was out there man. I can't believe there are places like that.

Village

December 1, 2019

I've been staying mostly in lately and just catching up on sleep. But last night I decided to exit... so I drifted off and when I felt the time was right I exited. As I was exiting though I felt a tremendous pull on my astral body and halfway out I was ripped from my physical body. This dark force took me away into an immense black void. I started praying for someone or something to get me out...

Then I saw a bright dust appear. As it spread beneath me I could suddenly tell they were the lights of a wooden village. Then there was a hill and a sky and I landed. It seemed to be twilight and I was at the bottom of a large forest hill. Below me I could see a beautiful little town with smoke chimneys going in the evening sky. I saw someone approaching... it was a man in a robe coming down the hill on a small dirt path. He looked Asian and wise. He stopped before me and I addressed him. "Are you a Master?" I asked hopeful I had stumbled unto a wizened being. "No," he said, "just out for a walk." He then proceeded down the hill toward the village. I followed...

I lost sight of the man but came upon a few people as I neared the village. They were sitting in a circle with a bowl in the middle. They called out to me to join them and I took a seat in the circle. Then, one of the girls reached into the pot in the middle and pulled out a small figurine of a dolphin. She threw it into the air and it exploded into a zillion particles. Next thing I know there are real live dolphins swimming around us yipping and yapping happy as can be. Everyone started laughing until they went away. We went through like 3 more figurines before I woke up. One was an octopus where octopuses appeared. Then there were sea horses and then sea stars. It was an interesting AP even though it started kind of bad.

The Grove

December 9, 2019

I became lucid as I was walking down a forest trail. Then I saw a grove of giant sequoia trees and looked up into their giant branches. It was so familiar to me and that's when I knew I had been here many times in my travels. It was like a big recollection... "Oh! The Grove!"

There where people there too that came out of the forest to greet me. I didn't just know them, I remembered having spent years with them here in "the Grove". This had been my home for a long time... maybe even before I had been born. There where many people who presented themselves to me and amazingly I knew most of their names. We played a little game where one by one someone came forward and it was my job to remember their name. Everytime i remembered correctly they would all clap and holler.

The Grove was like an astral park where souls would come replenish themselves. There was Eugene... our leader who took care of us and the Grove. We all took care of our beautiful forest. And there was a river where spirits would wade in to heal themselves. It was our job to guide the souls through the Grove (and the river) and make sure everyone was taken care of.

I met this special girl there that was instantly recognizable to me. I have never seen this person in real life but yet in the astral I remembered a long history of friendship between us. She came up to me at one point and said, "Do you remember me? We share a deep connection." And it was true... I totally felt for this girl and remembered her name.

We all gathered together and Eugene led us into the river. It was quite beautiful. I felt replenished. Then they all put on a show under the Grove with aerial acrobatics. There was a small audience of souls that had come to be healed and we all ah and oohed.

I woke up feeling like I had recovered a piece of my astral history. I hope I get to go back there again. I can't wait to see it again and have that Home feeling one more time.

Astral Television

December 14, 2019

There have been three attempts now at astral entities trying to teach me "astral television". First, you need the actual construct of the astral tv. Then you can join your spirit to it and let it develop. Well, last night I actually sat down to see what it was all about. I'd been resisting it because I didn't really want to share myself but I figured they were doing it too. So, I sat down watched an astral show with a few people.

It was a story about how we were all afraid of each other but that in the end we were all the same. The story developed from all people watching it. It was beautiful seeing us dream together and come to some unified understanding of ourselves.

So astral tv wasn't as bad as I thought it would be... but I still don't want to do it so often. I like the astral tv where I am alone the best. I think we all do... it reminds me of Brave New World where Alphas would get together to meditate and dream on Soma. It was done once in a while but not often. Still, it was beautiful...

Astral Egg

January 5, 2020

Last night, I sneaked out of body and slipped through my wall outside. In the grass was this egg that was shining. I was greatly curious so I picked it up. Something crazy happened however. I was sucked right inside the egg. Inside I saw amazing things.

It was better than astral tv. It was like an iPad egg with virtual apps and games. It was connected straight to my consciousness so I could pick which apps and games to play just by thinking about them.

They had all kinds of stuff! They had social apps that where like channels where people could hang out. They were like mini astral planes that led to other mini astral planes. But some weren't so small. Some were big planes like central hubs where a lot of traffic moved. These were like gateways to many other places.

But my iPad egg also had other apps. I launched the Astral Massage app and was taken into a place where there where beautiful soft shapes that my mind just glided into and it moved and rocked my being to ecstasy.

I played this crazy app... I think it was a game. I was on a boat and Orca whales are coming out of the mountains and splashing into the sea. One moved close and I start riding the whale as it zooms and zags at breakneck speed.

I launched out of the egg and pocketed it for further analysis.

Border of Hell

February 7, 2020

I woke up in the astral and went outside my house. Outside was the beach, literally. I didn't even have to walk... it was more of a glide. I floated about a foot off the ground and just flew where I wanted. This AP was one that let me experience what it would permanently feel to live in the astral - it lasted so long. First, I explored the beach and got lost in viewing all the people and phenomena. It seems I could float on water as well and that was fun. It seemed to be a twilight setting. At one point I went under a bridge and something got my immediate attention. It was like a sense of smell. And I smelled evil. The closer I got to land there, the more it stank and I could see hungry beings who were already trying to lure me further down to an astral hell. I quickly got out of there.

I traveled and traveled. I found some friends to hang out with and we hung out at this small ranch they had on a hill. It was nice talking in the astral and being around families again. Someone then asked me if I had gone to my Laying of the Rocks. I asked what that was... apparently it was the astral version of a trip to Mecca. But in this case it was a journey or pilgrimage to see God.

I was instantly interested so I went with my new friend and he dropped me off at the right plane. There was a field of rocks there and I was told to pick up the same number of rocks as I had serious questions for God. So in my case I picked two and put them in a sack. There must have been thousands of souls on their Laying of the Rocks.

We all started walking and walking and the more we made it into the inside plane I started to have second thoughts. The atmosphere had grown very serious. Not like a happy "let's go visit God" trip but a serious "Do I really want to mess around with God?" feeling. The closer we came to God the more this sense of serious power oozed from the very air. It was ominous.

I just got in line and followed everyone forward. Suddenly everything started shaking. Someone was explaining that it was normal to get rid of the rocks God thought where deemed petty or unnecessary. Remember, each rock represented a real serious question we wanted to see God about. Well, both my rocks disappeared. I guess they were not that serious to bother real God with. Some people, very few, were only left with one rock.

The size and raw power of God was making it-self very plain. At this point we were told we could go forward and seek our fates or turn back. Most of the people who wanted to see God turned back... and I was one of them. My astral body understood that this was a power not to play around with. Love and joy and the beautiful lighted planes would do fine. I didn't really need to confront God himself about my little life.

I flew back to my new friends and shared my experience. Apparently they had had a similar one. Like I said, apparently mostly everyone turns back from really meeting God.

I woke up and knew I immediately I had to get this down. I had a new experience of God - a new aspect of Him - and he was terrifying. That raw power that just makes you want to run away. I was sorry God took my rocks but I understand that I'm one of the lucky ones. There are people out there with serious problems and maybe that's what a God can do for them. I was surprised God was not a man but a huge infinite entity with infinite power. He was in this AP anyway.

There was one part I left out and will share... everyone gets a new name after the pilgrimage. It's actually considered a middle name. I still remember mine and it was written on a stone we all got after the decision to stop or go on. It was my full name but it had an extra middle name. I think I should keep it to myself.

Anyway, it was a big night and it taught me a lot about traveling and existing for hours lucidly in the astral. But mostly it taught me not to complain too much about my little problems. Amen.

Boy Scouts

March 11, 2020

Last night I had a real nice AP. It started with me getting out of body and walking out my front door. Even though it was 3 am in the real world, outside it was more like evening and it was a beautiful day. I felt like walking so I followed my sidewalk to a beautiful park. Everything was so green and there was a refreshing breeze which is rare. There were lots of people there enjoying the park. I sat on a swing set and just took it all in.

But it was getting kind of late. These two Boy Scouts came around and said the park was closing. Everyone was making their way to the entrance. I followed the crowd and started walking picking a path at random. I passed some kind of university, and the Boy Scouts headquarters which was odd. I passed a water park where I spent some time too. Then I found a movie theater with like 20 new movies showing. The posters were dazzling and I went in and watched part of a movie. It was about a girl and a boy on a hill and they were saying goodbye for the last time. The colors were absolutely brilliant and the screen was huge.

After a while I seemed to forget I was APing and just wanted to go home. But I couldn't find my way. I asked directions from two more Boy Scouts and they gave me a ride in their cool car. We picked up some fast food which was free on the way. Then they dropped me off at my astral home. Things finally started to look familiar. I went in and woke up.

Now here is the strange part... after waking up in the morning I make some coffee and go say good morning to my Mom. She's up and going through some of my childhood photos. She says, "Look hun, this is when you were little." She hands me a photo of me as a Boy Scout. Whoa! I felt like I was still dreaming. In fact maybe I didn't make it back all the way to waking on that last one. Anyway, definitely kind of deja-vu.

Astral Cigarette

March 16, 2020

I found a new way of exiting... I fell asleep and when I was ready to exit well, I just opened my eyes and I was outside my house. I didn't need to exit my body, or get out of bed, I just sort of trans-located. I'm going try it again tonight if I can.

Anyway, as soon as I was outside I took a look around my neighborhood. It was nighttime and the regular houses had been replaced by row and row of bars and restaurants. It was a festive atmosphere and I could hear some tune playing in the air.

What I did next was sort of explore. I went all the way down the street to where the road meets the main avenue. As soon as I got there, there were no lights, no activity, a dead zone. It felt like all the life was gone. It was so eerie. I was kinda spooked seeing that empty street. I went back to where the bars were having their party and I went inside one. There where some people at the bar and the tables. I sat down on a stool and started talking to this dude who offered me a cigarette. This was my second astral cigarette and it was just as enjoyable as the first - much more real and tasty than a real cigarette.

I woke up soon after that.

A Beautiful House

May 4, 2020

About an hour ago I woke up from a nice AP. I got out of body and off my bed and decided this time to explore my home and not go outside. The funny thing, after some exploring, is that my house in the astral was a luxurious house. It had three levels and my backyard was huge. And I could change things just by squeezing my fist. Things would transform into whatever I wanted and I seemed to have quite an imagination in the astral.

The backyard was full of neighbors having a bbq. I went out and joined them. We started talking but they all wanted to come in my house and check it out. So in they came against my wishes. Up the stairs and into my room were they lay down on the bed and fell asleep. Well, I woke them up and asked them to leave but they complained that my house was the best and they didn't want to go home. I offered to show them how to transform their own houses... so off we went to their house. There where like three of them, two boys and a girl.

It took about half an hour per house... in a few ways it was an exhausting AP. We found a trapped ghost in one house - the girl's - where a little girl lived in her closet. She didn't speak and we couldn't make her leave so we gave her some pillows and a blanket and left her be. We continued to make their houses really beautiful and luxurious over the next hours

After we were done with their houses which they did a great job on I came back to my house to find it in it's regal state. There was an elevator in the lobby which didn't used to be there so I took it to my third floor room and got into bed and went to sleep in my astral bed. Ahhhh, a job well done.

I think I slept for another hour dreaming about huge rooms with nebulas and galaxies in them.

A Thousand Voices

May 15, 2020

I had an interesting experience last night. I was sort of meditating in my large bean bag and I must of fallen asleep. I then became lucid and knew I was in the astral. I sorta lifted my upper body and then noticed that gravity was very low and drifted up and up into a black sky. It was expansive and I had a crystal clarity of this immense room I drifted up into.

There where voices in that silence that got more pronounced until I could hear thousands of voices talking over each other. Then voices became so numerous they became a white hum that had form and feeling. And then that ocean of awareness touched me on my left foot and sort of attached itself to my foot chakra. It was a weird feeling but very pleasant. - extremely pleasant actually. It felt like my foot was being massaged from the inside by the whole world.

I woke up and my foot was still humming with energy. It lasted like 20 minutes and then it faded. But for a while there it felt like... like... I had a hook-up to the cosmic internet and it plugged right into my foot. My foot was full of this amazing holy energy and awareness. I don't even have the words to describe this feeling but it hummed and just as it was affecting me, I could also affect it. It felt like someone had put a piece of pure Love right up my foot.

Father

May 29, 2020

Last night I had a lucid AP about my deceased father. We were at the family farm which is his favorite place to be and where he retired. We were sitting on the porch looking out toward the forested ravine where the orange groves are. I was totally lucid and here was my chance to talk to him finally.

I asked him if he knew he had died? And he said that of course he remembered his death. He went on to say that he had passed some kind of judgment or review of his life before he had been allowed to come here at the "farm". He said that he was definitely not dead in the sense of non-existence - that he had awareness and that he was learning how to exist in this new reality.

I really hope that this AP was not just a dream I dreamed to console myself that my father was not really dead. But now more than ever I think maybe he really is out there at the farm, drinking his beers and tending his orange groves. I hope so anyway.

Astral Sex

July 6, 2020

I used a fan last night to fall asleep. My air conditioner broke and they have yet to fix it. So I was using a fan and this, I believe, helped me exit my body into the astral. I climbed out of bed and I knew I was completely lucid in the astral. I went out my room and out the front door into the deep dark night.

I looked up and down our street. A few houses had lights on their porches and these are the ones I visit. I stay away from the dark houses and this has become a signal for me and my higher astral self to communicate and say yes, that house is safe. The house across the street had their lights on. So I hopped and floated across the street and went in. Houses are always unlocked in the astral.

My sight was super clear as I opened the door. Inside were four people. I quickly took stock of what was happening. Four people were dreaming and I said, "Hi Mother!" to the older woman there knowing she would then accept me in her dream. A smile crossed her face and then she went on cooking dinner.

I spied a beautiful girl on the couch and I went up to her, offered my hand, and said, "Let's go to your room." She smiled and took my hand and we retired to her room where I kissed her thoroughly and we lay on her bed for about 30 minutes doing what men and women do when they are alone together.

The sex was beautiful and as we lay locked in union, were transported to another world as we explored deep kisses and deep connection. I had never had astral sex this good... it lasted so long and was so deep. It definitely helped me clear the cobwebs that had accumulated over the past weeks. For some time now my astral travels had been boring and predictable... anyway, last night trumped all of that and I woke up refreshed and with a big smile on my face.

Trionomy

July 7, 2020

I was lucid but I don't remember how it had started. I was with my brother and his friend and we were going into the university to get our Trionomy books. Everyone was learning Trionomy. I wasn't too sure I cared or actually didn't understand what the big deal was... but it was new and gathering quite a following.

In the back of my mind I wondered if living in the astral could support such things as universities and book learning. I decided to closely pay attention.

We followed the crowds into this large room with tables. On the tables were the books on Trionomy. We got in line and soon we each had our own copy. My brother's friend was really excited because as he put it, "It's the next level!"

My brother and friend then departed or at least I lost track of them. I sat down on a bench and leafed through my new book on Trionomy. There where some diagrams that looked interesting but in the end I thought this was probably just the latest fad in human astral dynamics. That's when a cute mousey blond girl sat next to me. We got into a conversation and she wanted to know all my fields of expertise. I rattled off all the computer languages I knew and she seemed impressed. I took a chance and kissed her lightly on her tiny mouth. She smiled and kissed me right back.

"But how good are you at Trionomy?" she asked with a mischievous smile. Hmmm... I should of really found out what Trionomy is.

Hippy Festival

July 16, 2020

It all started late last night. It was around 3 am when I finally stopped my reading and fell asleep. At some point I became lucid and rolled out of my bed into the astral. I went outside and that's how my adventure began.

Outside it was dark but not pitch. A blue and purple light ebbed from the sky and there where pale and thin wisps of clouds with a starry background beneath. In my back yard I found an old lady looking up at the sky. She had a pair of ear phones on which attached to a small dish which was pointed upwards to the heavens. I asked her what she was doing.

"I'm listening to the Changes," she said. "There's something happening to the world and if you listen carefully you can hear it." I moved on down the street and passed a store where they were selling ear phones and dishes. It was packed with people. People where coming out with their brand new ear phones and dishes. It was really interesting and it seemed to be some kind of global phenomena happening. I continued down the street.

I came to a wonderful place. It was some kind of hippy festival and flea market. I immediately went in. There where lots of people enjoying the festival and selling and buying things. I passed stalls of masks and jewelry, wood carvings, incense and spices, furniture, herbs and smoking supplies, and all kinds of stalls selling foods. It was really cool and I spent most of my time looking at things and tasting the local cuisine. I had my wallet with me and it was loaded with money. When I offered them my money they seemed surprised I was using dollars but accepted them nonetheless. I was offered some kind of edible for free and I ate it and it made me feel really good.

I also had a cell phone with me and one point it started making weird sounds. I took it out of my pocket and the screen was saying the gps location was something like Aurora. I've never heard of a city called Aurora myself but I was in the astral. Then a red alarm came on it and said that cell phones were not allowed here in Aurora and then it started to morph. It turned into this little aquarium with a tiny little fish swimming inside it. It was really pretty. I put it back in my pocket and walked on.

I came upon this work of art. The art was actually a large stairs that led down to the beach. It's so hard to describe these stairs... it was like fronds that curved down in sections and they were all kinds of colors. I took the fronds down to the beach and sat down with my bag which was full of stuff I had bought at the hippy festival.

The sun started to come up and eventually I woke up. I really had a good time.

<u>Meditating Monks</u>

August 1, 2020

Last night I exited into my room and then went outside. It was a beautiful night. I activated my hand jets and rose into the air. Instead of going down the street like I sometimes do, I went straight up toward a bank of clouds that peeped pink and orange from the sunset. What I saw above to clouds surprised me.

Hovering in between the clouds where hundreds of meditating monks. I could see the closest ones with their eyes wide open and strangely lit looking toward a point deep inside themselves.

I waited a few seconds, just hovering there in the starry night breeze, to see what would develop.

Just as I began to get bored this sense of peace and wholeness overtook me. Something pushed me from below. It felt like a cushion of air. I slowly settled and turned my hand jets off. I was floating. Levitating.

I breathed in deeply. I had never felt so at peace. The mediating monks seemed to be sharing their vibration with me. I felt safe, serene, awake, and safe. My breath was the best part of it. It felt like all of us where breathing in-sync. There has never been a place I most wanted to be and most want to return to. It felt amazingly beautiful as if I had been searching for such a place all my life.

At the same time it felt like it was the most ordinary thing to do. As if this amazing peace was the default setting of the Universe. No matter what happened to me I now knew that I could return to this place anytime I wanted.

To test this I meditated this morning and visualized myself in those clouds, surrounded by all the peaceful monks. The feeling returned. It was so simple and yet it was everything I had been searching for.

It might sound boring, just sitting and sharing silence in the clouds but something maintains us. It's almost like a blanket of Love surrounds us all and as is still and quiet and we wouldn't want to be anywhere else.

I surmise that we can tap into this vibration anytime we want. Have you every meditated in a group? Well, same thing. All we need to do is connect to all those beautiful beings that are now serenely meditating and become one of them. The more the merrier! Ahhhh!

Ex-girlfriend

August 5, 2020

It was a pleasant lucid dream last night but also a little sad. All I remember was that I was being escorted down this hallway in a really modern building. Everything was clean in shades of blue. In fact, the color blue was everywhere. The person escorting me was a black female with a spiffy little suit.

We turned a corner and entered an empty room. Inside was a black man in his own spiffy suit and my ex-girlfriend. She seemed to be glowing and her blond hair shown clean, long, and bright. Her vivid blue eyes shown as she looked at me with this small little sad smile.

The black woman was suddenly asking me a question. "Do you want her?" I said, "No. She broke my heart." It was over just as quick as that and we left the room and my escort disappeared.

I walked out unto this balcony that overlooked a huge fruit tree. I remember how me and my ex had walked under that same huge tree in happier days. Now I could see that the fruit had been harvested and the color of it was darker. I could see the empty pods where the fruit had been.

All I remember next is that I spent the rest of my dream looking for my ex-girlfriend. I think I had changed my mind and was asking everyone in a suit where she was. She was nowhere to be found.

Mining Town

August 12, 2020

Last night was really amazing. I decided on a long trip... a journey "out there". I got out of my body and started flying. Straight up I went for like what seemed 15 minutes. I saw space, and stars, and galaxies. I kept going and going with the intention to find something beautiful. Then... Bump... I found it.

Out of the mists appeared a mountain. I flew above it looking down at the most charming mountain village. It was sizable though with pretty little white washed brick houses with pretty little red roofs. Toward the center of the community rose some really modern looking buildings that contrasted yet complimented the town.

I flew down toward the building and found an open window. Some lady greeted me with surprise and invited me inside. She was friendly enough but was really surprised. In a matter of minutes they came to arrest me. I was taken down to the town and processed. They asked a lot of questions and I told then that I was just exploring the Universe when I found them.

They weren't mean at all. I think they were shocked to see me as if they hardly get any visitors. My astral body was given a medical exam and I was given a few injections and some kind of energy treatment. Afterwards I felt really good. They gave me a uniform and eventually someone picked me up. I had been assigned to one of the processing stations. My boss was some dude or other that explained to me that they're little town surrounds a hot pocket of some kind of energy they mine.

This had all taken a really long time and I just wanted to wake up but I couldn't. I was starting to get worried. The way they acted was like I didn't have a body waiting for me back on Earth. They had no idea I was just projecting. To them I was an outsider that miraculously had found them and their little operation. I was processed and made part of the community.

But I still couldn't wake up. I started thinking maybe I had severed my connection with my body somehow or they had.

Still, this wasn't the worst place to land. Everything looked clean and bright and everyone looked really attractive. After the tour of my job I was given quarters and some free time. I visited a gorgeous little park with lots of friendly and happy people. They were flying around, having picnics, dancing, and enjoying themselves. At one point a found a small hole in the ground and looked inside. It was full of stars and I wondered if these little stars were what they mined here at this outpost somewhere out there in the astral.

I remember thinking that my astral body had never felt so good and healthy. Whatever they had done to me at their hospital I felt great. I felt the awareness of not just my astral body but other finer bodies beneath that. I knew for the first time that astral bodies are just one of finer and finer bodies we all have. And like our physical body maybe sometimes they need to be maintained.

So anyway... I was at that park when I had to go pee. But astral bodies don't pee right? That's when I realized that the feeling had been creeping up on me from Earth where my physical body needed to urinate. I concentrated really hard and

I was suddenly in my bed - awake! I went to the bathroom to relieve myself.

I was back but I felt really different. The physical world almost seemed like a dream. I was sure I was back but not 100% sure. Kind of like an astral hang-over.

Astral Drugs

August 14, 2020

It was definitely a guided AP because it started just like a movie with a short intro. The intro was just like a documentary that explained that humans are spiritual beings and they have the ability to incorporate new energy into their systems. Being human and rotating around our specific star only allows us to have certain genes which can only access certain energies. It said that a lot of humans do drugs because of this reason especially drugs with helper or ally energy. However, using these types of allies and helpers can sometimes lead us into problems because of their course nature.

I think what it was trying to say was don't use them cheap human drugs! Use ours! They are designed from the ground up to be real helpers and allies to your system. The lucid dream began!

This nice human was blowing smoke over my face and I quickly went to a semi trance state. I had an amazing vision of the cosmos as I felt myself being moved into the right astral plane. "I want that one!" I said to him. He laughed like a familiar grandfather and said, "That's nothing... just to get you there."

The next thing I know I was coming out of my trance and I was in this semi dark room. Some people were walking around trying the different allies one could get for your system. There where also some helper people walking around helping people.

I got into this conversation with this friendly person and he said to try "SpacePie 9". So I went up to one of the helpers and asked for that ally. He led me to this alcove where a pair of simple ear phones stuck out of the wall. There was also a nice bouncy chair. I hit play and I was off!

It was so much better than any drug I've ever done. I can't even describe this sensation and vision I had. It was cosmic! And it lasted forever. It was eternal. I woke up too soon because I had to go pee but from what I experienced it described not just a vision but knowledge that my system digested.

It was a super cool AP. I hope to go there again and try some of the other helpers and ally visions. There where tons!

Rave Party

August 22, 2020

I went to sleep early. I really wasn't sure I was deep enough to attempt an exit so I just rolled off the bed. When I didn't hit the floor I knew. I kept falling and falling. When I opened my eyes I was floating in a murky aqua-blue space. Time to go somewhere... I concentrated and felt my feet hit the ground... at a rave party!

It looked like a circular building with its center hollowed out. Some sort of arena. There was flashing lights and trance music booming through the air. Well I danced some and kissed a pretty girl and then thought I saw a friend from high-school. When I caught up with him he had no idea who I was... but it was him or his twin. Anyway, I left the astral party and walked out into the beyond. I found a nice tree and sat down on the grass and watched people go by. Most where like me and had left the party and had found a nice place to rest. The stars where out and as I looked up into the sky... something moved.

A little star was moving up there and then it started growing and coming closer to me. When it finally arrived I could see it was some kind of ufo. It was like a disc with its sides shorn off. It landed next to me and it spoke! "Climb on top and I'll take you up. You don't belong here." Ok... so I climbed on top of this grey disc with lights and up we went!

It climbed and climbed and I held on for dear life - up through the clouds into the heavens beyond.

When it landed it was in front of a really beautiful modern building. Someone was there waiting for me. Well, it was a long dream so I'll sum up. He led me into this building where I met a group of people and an older man who was some teacher or master. He told us all that he was going to teach us to change color and element.

First we learned how to change into liquids and the color blue. Each element came with a sensation and it's own unique qualities. Then there was fire, air, and space. I liked fire and I liked space even more. Space was a black color and there where ravens who joined us in that quality. I flew down a long dark tunnel being space which then turned me into a raven.

It was totally neat being in a different element. I woke up soon after that.

Astral Environments

September 3, 2020

I have an ongoing theory that the astral is populated by semi-permanent structures that serve as many of the environments. I also have a theory as to how they first come to exist. They are made by people or groups of people who are proficient in "weaving" astral matter together.

I APed tonight, exited, and went outside to my neighborhood. I went inside a random house just to see what was inside. Well, it served as a gateway to one of these astral environments.

It was huge and completely deserted. Some parts looked like the inside of a mall. There was a great empty theater that looked kind of eerie all by itself. I really wondered where I was. I could see no sky... it was all inside with drab walls and ceilings.

Then on one wall I saw a knob. Under the knob was a metal plate. I turned this big knob and lights started popping on. Then people appeared. When I had turned it all the way to the right, there was a full swinging party going on. Somehow turning that knob had phased me into the right level where the crowds where located.

I wandered around this mall and there where music and lights and groups of people dancing and store fronts where they sold clothes and knick-knacks. I bumped into these two girls who I think immediately knew I was new at this because they had this prankish look and started to follow me around saying things like, "Come here pretty boy, we won't hurt you." ...but all mischievous and laughing. Oh oh.

Anyway, I ran away and went into this other room. I think it was a sex den. I saw lots of people there cavorting and having group sex. I didn't find it at all attractive so I moved on.

I eventually found a gateway. It was a doorway with a screen next to it and touchpad. I quickly flipped through the screens and one said "If you'd like to provide a suggestion you can mail us here: The Sigma Group, Level I, and some numbers or something." One of the pages had a map of the Solar System and it had a picture of Earth which was Section F. I clicked on Section F for Earth and stepped through the gateway.

Section F was a farce of planet Earth. It was like a ride or show of someone's idea of Earth. It was NOT painted in a lovely light. It had displays of people chained up and going to work everyday and the boss cracking his whip. These where displayed on screens as you rode this train through this tunnel. It was like a Disney ride. Message: Earth is a slave planet where they keep their citizens in a proverbial cage and make them work for food. I don't know... there was something about that.

I don't remember much else except I found the gateway again and travelled to a nicer plane this time. I basically floated in space with a large group of people and we were all in sync as really good feelings wafted the space around us. It was really neat actually. It felt communal and clean with an aqua-blue light everywhere.

Playmates

September 13, 2020

Something very interesting has been happening the past three nights. I've had playmates! It started with me APing and going outside two nights ago. I was flying around the roof tops doing aero-acrobatics when I saw another person doing the same. I got a quick look at her for a second before she vanished.

Then, yesterday night I APed and went outside and found that same girl but she was waiting outside my house around the corner. She seemed shy and sort of pulled away when I approached her. I did manage to ask her name which she replied "Rafaela". She then flew off. A group of Latin Americans enjoying the night air and flying just like me then joined me and told me that Rafaela was shy but very friendly once you get to know her. There were two more girls and a guy. They all seemed young and vibrant... but I've never seen an old person in the astral.

Then tonight all my new friends where waiting for me when I went outside... including Rafaela. They showed me this cool technique on how to AP from an AP into a higher band or astral level. You can go to sleep in an already ongoing AP and AP again or you can use these cool gadgets that plug into your ears and sorta buzz. I learned a lot from them tonight and then we all four or five of us got into a astral car and went joy riding.

Land Time Forgot

September 24, 2020

I haven't APed in about 10 days. I've just been tired and decided to stay in mostly so I've just gone to sleep. But last night I decided to go out so I set myself up and performed an exit. I'm glad I did.

I got off my bed, already in the astral, and went outside. I hoped to see some houses with lights on because the utter darkness really creeps me out. I saw no lights this time however. I was a bit disappointed but decided not to waste my time. I launched into the air activating my hand jets since gravity was on.

I flew up and up looking for some lights. I flew away from my house and then my neighborhood. Suddenly the darkness receded and that omnipresent lighting appeared. It was like daytime now and I could see everything below. I landed in a very strange place.

I really took a chance to investigate the astral environment. It was AMAZING. It looked like a land time had forgotten. Everything was so sharp and steady and I used the trick Carlos Castaneda spoke about in his Dreaming. You sort of look at something but only for a few seconds. Then you change your view and do it again taking quick peeks around you. In this way you can get a very good look at the astral environment without things misting over and melting into something else. Well, I walked and walked and looked and looked. The astral is a WIERD place.

It looked like a whole bunch of different environments smashed together. There where streets. Some were paved, some where dirt. Some areas looked like the country and some the city. I saw an old mill with a broken down water wheel, old forgotten cars and buses from the 1940s, a field with old tents from medieval times, old messy alleyways between dilapidated buildings, everything old and ancient - forgotten. It felt like this was a place old astral environments came to die and be forgot. It was so eerie and not a soul or living thing around, just me. The color of it was almost gray like ash. And the detail of things! Little pebbles on the ground, an old rusty tomato soup can, an old boat engine, old newspapers, wooden little huts with doors coming off the hinges... you get the picture. Old... forgotten... lost.

Anyway, I really enjoyed it because my vision was extra clear and I got a chance to really perceive an astral world. It was beautiful in its own way, with that beauty that comes with exquisite astral vision.

Lonely Tacos

October 5, 2020

I fell asleep watching the movie Ad Astra on tv. I happened to AP and it sort of all got mixed up... because in the astral Brad Pitt was leading me down a path that lead to beautiful Alaska. The trees were so green and the simple dirt path was beautiful on both sides with wilderness. You could even taste the cool air and got my first sensation of astral temperature. It was cooler as we walked into the mountains. We arrived at a beautiful city high in the astral.

Brad Pitt seemed to vanish and I was left to explore the city. It was glacial with modern looking curves and designs. I found the theater and watched one of their movies. I got so high watching that movie that I don't remember much of it... but there was a boy and a girl and a wise person.

I went out of the theater after the movie and decided to go back to Earth. I walked down the mountains but the path became a river of mud making it impassable. I was trapped in the mountains without being able to wake up. I went back to the city and it was getting dark. People where disappearing. It was cold and lonely. I found a mom and her daughter selling tacos and they offered me some. It was yummi astral food.

I walked around in the dark and couldn't wake up. I started to wonder where people went to after dark. The streets of this city in the mountains where deserted. Maybe they have hotels? I don't remember much after that as I walked into the darkness...

Observations #2

October 23, 2020

I've been APing a lot lately. It started about a week ago. I think it had built up to the point where I had to get out. So I've been exploring the neighborhood... my astral neighborhood. Sometimes when I exit, it's dark, sometimes day, sometimes dawn, and dusk. Well I started to go into the houses more to see who is inside or where they lead. The weird thing is that none of the doors are ever locked. It's almost like a plastic or quantum version of my neighborhood.

Some houses have people inside them. Like a normal family doing their thing. But you can tell they are dreaming because they have this far off look in their eyes. If I find a house with a very attractive girl I will usually go up to her and try to start something. I've never had one turn me down... which means they are dream entities or humans are very loving creatures.

Some houses serve as gateways to other environments and sometimes they wisk me away to other parts of the Astral. Some environments are communal and for recreation. I think there are more real people than dream entities at some environments. Some places are completely deserted though and can range from completely disordered to beautiful gardens of infinite variety. My favorite was a Massage Room where you went in and the walls just hugged you in loving embraces and cuddling you with love energies.

What freaks me out a little is when I exit unto a night level and the houses are dark with no lights on any of them. I think I went into a dark house once and it was a very dark and quiet place. These places are isolated and really anything could be lurking so outside the Light. Not entirely negative but set aside to forget.

But then I have a lucid dream that makes all the darkness disappear... I think this is my higher-self and he'll drop by from time to time and surprise me. Surprises are always fun.

UFO to Another World

November 9, 2020

Last night I had a very nice astral projection. I went to sleep and was able to exit soon after. I went outside and that's when I saw the UFO for the second time. The last time I had seen it was November 27th 2019. I remember because that's the night my kitty got run over. That night I had APed and saw this huge UFO come down from the sky. Well I saw that same UFO last night. I had met some of the astral humans who lived inside it including their leader. He came down this plank and invited me inside the UFO. I was so excited to go with them.

At some point I asked them where we were going and he said we were picking up a friend of mine. The UFO took off and I settled in. I remember having a few conversations with some people I had met before on their last visit. Well, soon we landed again and up the ramp comes my dear friend Jessica. We used to work together at a videogame studio. We kind of skirted around a romantic relationship but eventually decided to keep things friendly - we've been pals ever since. She's into Buddhism and stuff. So after a joyful reunion we got into the UFO and off we went into the astral heavens.

They took us to visit their amazing civilization. It was a city and the UFO landed atop a cliff that overlooked it. It was beautiful and layed out in geometric precision next to a purple ocean. In the sky above was a layer of clouds with all kinds of lights flashing. At one point me and Jessa were asked to take out our "eggs" which were these small astral devices. I had almost forgotten I had mine because I hardly ever dream about it. I found it outside my house a long time ago in the grass. It's like an egg with astral apps and it can transport you to many different astral programs.

We were asked to dial a special program on our eggs and we then immediately found ourselves in a cloudy environment with a huge machine in the middle. It looked like a huge computer with all kinds of panels and wires that hooked up to two chairs with a device that fits over the head. We were asked to sit in these two chairs (Jessica and me) and told that this was a very special machine. What it did was use one's innate ability to find new frequencies in the great abstraction of the astral. These new frequencies are very special because their energy can be used to construct new objects and environments that can be explored and further our knowledge of the Spirit.

So me and Jessa get into these two chairs and they hook us up and boom they flip the on switch. I can't explain what we did together because it's so abstract. But it felt like a single particle representing my essence and a single particle representing Jessica's essence came together and started fluxing together. This fluxing gave off this electricity and the machine sort of skimmed the center of this electrical dance and extracted the very essence of our shared communion. It was over too quickly (because it was very pleasurable) and the machine stopped flashing and was still. In a little alcove of the machine was a tiny new little light. This was the new particle or singularity me and Jessa had created out of our energy dance. We were told to touch our eggs to it and this would seal a new app to our eggs - one that we could take with us and explore together or on our own. This, they said, was what they made new astral technology from including devices and new environments. These substances were very precious because they came from our essential natures.

After that me and Jessica were introduced to this older couple who taught us the basics of astral living. They basically gave us a crash course of how to levitate objects how to pull and push and manifest astral objects. This was my favorite part of the whole AP really... working and playing with my friend. We hovered several objects and even lifted a huge piano together and then learned how to draw on walls using nothing but mental powers. It was tons of fun and we laughed through out it.

Sarcophagus

November 19, 2020

I went to sleep and woke up in a completely different bedroom. That's when I knew I was in an astral projection. I looked around and it was my old bedroom in my old house when I was a teenager. I got out of bed and went outside using the back porch door.

As soon as I went outside I was floating. It was like gravity didn't exist for me. I floated up the small hill unto the road and around the bend. It was dawning and still a bit dark. I saw a nice pond and floated right unto it. I was afraid I'd get wet but I managed to steer my way clear and back unto the road. It was fun floating above water.

There was a nondescript house there with its second story window open. Right inside the window was a cute black and white kitty. I petted it while still floating outside and it started purring. It knew I was there and liked being pet. I floated down to the ground and went inside the house by opening the front door which was unlocked.

Inside everything was clean and pretty. The entrance led to a living room with a nice couch. I did not see any modern appliances however. I explored some more and found the stairway to the second story. It sort of circled around in an arc as it ascended. Above I found something super interesting.

It was all quiet and deserted. Maybe everyone was asleep so I hesitated to go into the closed rooms. Finally I chose a door and on the other side was a huge Egyptian sarcophagus. I don't think it was made of gold but I had the thought it was some eccentric guy's (or woman's) version of a bed. The lid was closed though. On the walls were all kinds of Egyptian writing. There was all kinds of art everywhere. It was so detailed! I found a bathroom and it was a huge tub with statues on the walls. The spigot was a beautiful naked woman pouring from a vase.

I backtracked and this time I saw people. In one of the main rooms around a big table were several people arguing. They were all dressed in black pajamas. One man was yelling or gesticulating to the others but I couldn't hear them. And for some reason they couldn't see me.

A little apart was a couch and a lovely girl was sitting there. She looked troubled like she didn't like the other people arguing. She was very lovely... so I leaned in and kissed her. As I pulled back her hand went to her lips like she had felt it but not seen me. I woke up right after that.

Ape Men

December 17, 2020

I fell asleep on my bean bag and so it was a bit awkward getting up. I looked back at my large bean bag and there was no body. Actually it's been awhile since I've seen my body when I exit. It only happens rarely now. To make sure I was in the astral I engaged my hand jets and started flying in my room floating around. I went right through the wall and then I was outside.

I looked up and down the street for any lights or anything odd. It was mostly dark with all the houses slumbering in the deep dark night. Only one building had their lights on so I headed toward it. On closer examination it appeared to be an arcade with many game machines showing through the window. Next to the entrance were two gorgeous women talking. I was tempted to talk to them but instead went inside the arcade.

Inside was a bouncer who looked kind of tough and checked me out. Before letting me in he said he had to do a scan. He took my hands and held them for like 15 seconds. He then said, "You have to come with me." I was immediately suspicious. I asked him why he had scanned me or done whatever he did and he said, "You shouldn't have asked that." I really didn't know what was going on at that point.

We headed down a corridor. I saw some tables with a few couples eating dinner. We came to a room and the bouncer said, "We've transported your team, they are inside. Just wait until someone comes to get you." I went inside and found four of my old buddies from work. They seemed kind of confused what they were doing there. After a little conversation we established that most of us had just gone to sleep and had been ripped from our respective dreams.

A door in the back opened and out came this crazy looking ape man in a robot suit! He was followed by four more ape men who began beating their chests at us. Someone finally came and explained that the game was about to begin. We were led out into a huge arena with thousands of people cheering. It seemed we were expected to play basketball against the five ape men! I just went with it and led my team unto the court. The game started and we were off all of us getting into the spirit of the game.

The ape men were really good basketball players and embarrassed our team to the laughter of the crowd. I felt a little embarrassed and chagrined as they played circles around us. I think I got the ball only once and scored only one time before I woke up back to my bean bag in bewilderment. Strange huh? Those ape men were really freaky!

Finding a Soul

December 21, 2020

I had a very strange one last night. It was kind of scary but ultimately inspiring for me. I became lucid in a green, green, forest. I was traipsing through the chaparral looking for my ex-girlfriend's house. I had this sense of urgency like something was wrong and I just had to see her. Somehow I knew that her house was somewhere in these woods. The color green was very vivid everywhere.

After searching and searching I saw something in the woods. It was a quaint little trailer like a mobile home or RV. It was really cute and above the door were the numbers 11111. But something was the matter... that sense of something being wrong came to the forefront. As I inspected the cute trailer I saw that the door was hanging off its hinges. And then I could see the footprints. They looked like lizard footprint all around the little vehicle. I steeled myself and approached. I opened the door and went in!

Inside it was a big mess. Things had been thrown about and shattered objects littered the floor. In one corner was this person that looked like some sort of demon. He had a black hat on and this devilish grin. And he was dirty with half rotten skin. But there was no sign of my girlfriend. The demon started laughing and laughing. I yelled at it to get out and it turned into a dark mist that sped out the door.

I went outside and found this thin white thread that was tied to the trailer. I followed it a short distance into the forest and found the other end tied to a stick. I knew instinctively that my girlfriend's soul was buried under there and I had to deliver it safely back to her. I dug and found it. It was a collection of three small objects. One object was a very green marble with all kinds of kaleidoscope patterns. Another one was a shiny silver knob of a branch where three twigs came together. And the last object was the most delicate butterfly wing all done in pink. I pocketed the objects and went to find my girlfriend.

She was at this school taking a class. It was like a giant tree-house with desks inside. I stormed in yelling her name but couldn't find her. Then I heard her sweet voice, "Here I am!" I have never been so glad to find anyone. I knew then that she was going to be alright.

I explained to her what I had found lurking at her house and how I had banished the demon. I took out a bag and laid out some treasures and gifts I had found at her place. Then I told her I had found her soul and that it was safe. I took out the small bag with her soul in it and gave it to her.

And that's when I woke up really suddenly! It was the middle of the night and my neighbor's dog was going crazy! Bark bark bark! Howl howl howl! I got up and grabbed my flashlight and looked out the porch door windows. For some reason the dog was going nuts. I saw my neighbor come out and look around the yard for a prowler. Eventually the dog calmed down and I got back in bed and fell back asleep. I still have no idea why the dog started barking but it felt like an omen that it chose that particular instant. The instant I had laid my girlfriend's soul into her hands.

Hap 8 Hab

January 3, 2020

I was slumbering in my bean bag when I found myself able to exit. Why not? I performed my phase and in seconds I was in the astral. Getting up from my bean bag is always awkward but I finally managed to get up and perform a centering so that I wouldn't wake up again. Finally when I was grounded in the astral I headed outside.

It was daytime and the sky was so dang blue - miles of blue without one cloud in it. The houses looked brand new and bright with all kinds of color. The lawns looked like they had been manicured to perfection and the grass was so green. The pavement on the street also looked brand new and so shiny. It reflected the sky so the roads looked blue too! It was so beautiful that I just floated there outside my house for a long while looking at everything. There weere no cars anywhere and the entire neighborhood looked deserted. It was breathtaking.

I started my explorations by floating down the street and around the corner looking for that anomaly that just begs to be explored. Every AP has one or more. I turned another corner and aha! A car was parked in one of the houses! Anomaly! I approached the house and saw that the car was a Thunderbird. On the front door was a post-it with handwritten writing. It said "hap 8 hab". I don't have a clue what means. Anyway, I opened the door and went in.

Inside it was nice and shady - a contrast from the bright outside. There was a living room that had a television playing the strangest commercials. I watched for a while. Three people where exploring a cave on TV and they were talking in a foreign language. They had these long one piece suits and they where flying around the cave. Astral television for astral worlds I guess.

I explored some more and found a bedroom with a door open. I looked inside and there was this woman sitting up in her bed! It was so eerie. She was kind of pretty with white skin and dark hair. She was about 30ish and she just looked at me for awhile. Well, I suddenly felt like my temperature rose and so I did the natural thing and joined her in bed. She smiled this little smile that said something like, lucky me! And then we were together.

It just makes me wonder where these worlds really are and why they are so real. It's definitely an area that needs to be explored. It's another world!

Being an Alien

January 13, 2021

Last night was my record breaker for strange APs! I went to sleep after meditating for a little and making a small prayer for an interesting AP. Well last night I got one. I went to sleep and after a few minutes performed an exit. And a very strange journey began...

I did not exit into my room as usual. As I rolled out of bed I could tell this was not my room or my house. Looking about and outside the windows I could see I was in some kind of apartment high in the sky. Outside was a beautiful city with all its lights on. I must have been on the 79th floor in some downtown apartment. Everything looked so nice and clean.

There was a man there I met or rather an alien who spoke to me and said we had to go downtown to where all new visitors first stay. He was very nice and asked me questions like my name and where I came from. The alien had no face but just 5 lines that spiraled around his face. And yet sometimes I would see a regular face like a human being. Anyway, we made it downtown where I was put in this big room with a few others. I remembered I was asked what my interests where and people kept coming up to me to ask who I was.

I found a computer and started playing with it. If I had to guess I would say that their level of computing technology was around our 1985 with 8-bit color. A man asked me if I was interested in computers and he asked me if I'd like to learn how to program them. I could swear he took the face of my brother for a moment. It was so sincere and lacked all deceit. So I went with him.

What followed where like 2 days where I learned to live in this new civilization. I went to a house and had my own room and computer where I learned how to make astral games to sell. People would use some kind of astral internet to trade games and movies. They had money or some kind of credit system. That's when I learned that this was a medium-small astral civilization. New people were constantly coming in and so the best way was to set them up with a skill set and place to live. I had been recruited myself by a game creator who taught me how to make the games.

I think a lot of the people there had been around a long time. It felt like a swinging and happening civilization was underway.

They had a funny way of eating even. I still don't understand but every time it was meal time a huge section of space would detach itself from the abstract. To feed you had to find the central cell of this section. Food came out of there like a warm honey. It tasted kind of good. I really don't understand what the eating was about but everyone was having meals like regular. Wierd huh?

Looking in a mirror I could see I was a short little alien too. When I woke up several long hours later into Earth time I felt like I didn't belong in my human shape. I felt a little alien still. It lasted about 2 hours this weird feeling of having been a different form.

Anyway, this brought home how weird the astral can be and those amazing other orders of reality.

Magazine Girl

January 24, 2021

I was drowsing and I slipped sideways into an astral projection. I had been laying down on the couch and then I had passed the boundary and I was in the astral. I was sitting down in a chair looking at a beautiful room. The house was my aunt's house and it looked sparkling clean. There where red drapes in the corners and it looked like it had undergone a makeover. I was in the living room of this big house and I spied a magazine with a beautiful girl on the cover. For some reason it shone with attention. I focused on it and suddenly there was a small miniature figurine about a foot high of this girl. She was dressed in a pretty dress with a short skirt and she looked beautiful.

She was alive moving and looking at me with deep blue eyes. I wished most of all that she was bigger so knowing I was in a lucid dream I wished her Big! She grew to three feet and said, "Make me bigger." So I wished again and then she was in a small alcove in the corner. A curtain was drawn half-way over this small space and inside was the most beautiful girl I've ever seen. I pushed the curtain aside and there was a 5 foot version of the magazine girl.

I learned quite a few things from this girl. She was some kind of dream manifestation. When I asked her why she looked so much like my ex-girlfriend she didn't say anything but we were suddenly linked by some psychic connection. She was at once completely my dream and my ex-girlfriend all at once. There was no conflict between her and me. It felt like she would do anything for me. And in exchange I would love her completely. It was beautiful. We went on to do some intimate things.

Suddenly I hear, "Honey, would you like a sandwich? I can make you one..." I turned around and it was my mother calling from the kitchen. I was still in the astral though and my Mom was there. I said goodbye to my girlfriend and went to deal with my mother.

"Common Mom, let's go outside." I took my Mom outside and we went into the street.

Outside it was a beautiful city at mid-afternoon. The buildings looked regal with very nice architecture. My mother suddenly had a camera and was shooting pictures of the city. It was kind of funny. And then I looked about and she had disappeared. Gone. I always wondered what I would look like waking up in the middle of a dream to someone else. Now I know... they just vanish.

I went back to the house to look for my girlfriend but as I walked into the front porch I could see that it had been taken over by lots of people. There was a table with 5 people playing poker. There was a man with a rifle in shades in the corner that looked like he belonged to a guerrilla outfit. And there were some skateboarders wasting time near the entrance.

I was a bit disappointed that my dream had been colonized. I woke up right after that.

I went to get some coffee to wake up, and my real Mom is in the kitchen. And she says, "You want a sandwich honey? What can I make you?" I kind of freaked out. Makes me think that physical reality is just another astral plane or our reality may not be as solid as we might think.

Sphere 1159

February 1, 2021

I went to sleep with the intention of APing but had a tough time exiting my body. I kept waking up. On my third attempt I was slowly able to exit without breaking the spell. I immediately went outside and saw that it was nighttime in the astral with long puffy clouds moving through the sky. I took flight and floated down the street looking for something interesting. The houses in the neighborhood suddenly vanished and a field followed by a hill presented itself. I flew over the hill and there was the ocean as far as the eye could see. The water was aqua color with a glow all of its own.

For some reason gravity was becoming an issue. I began to sink and plop went right into the ocean. For a split second I saw a door in the water and then I was in the water. I got sucked down into the depths.

As suddenly as that, I was rolling down a hill like I had been spit out. At the bottom I came to a highway where cars were going by very fast. Some of them beeped at me. It was nighttime but I could see that the cars where no ordinary cars. They all looked to be the same model and they were small and boxy. I started walking down the highway wondering where the heck I was when one of the cars stopped. Someone rolled down the window and asked, "Are you lost?"

I explained I was astral projecting and they asked where I was from. I said I was from Florida and they said they had never heard of it. "Well you shouldn't really be out here in the middle of the night. Common, we'll give you a ride into town." I got into their car and off we went. There weere two girls and a male driver. They appeared to be human. In the car I asked them where I was and the driver said, "You are on P Sphere 1159." (What kind of a crazy astral place is this? I asked myself.)

Well we went to like a cop station where they explained I was lost and that I needed someone to take me back to my own astral plane. Someone with know how was summoned and I was put in his charge. He was wearing loose fitting clothing all in black. Well I followed him and we went through a maze of astral planes until we crossed a sea and a hill and there was my neighborhood. We landed next to my house where I thanked the nice man and went inside. As soon as I was in my room I woke up!

Soldiers

February 13, 2021

Last night I was trying to AP and I must have gone to sleep and missed my window because I don't remember an exiting sequence. However, I found myself lucid soon after and I knew I had made it to the other side. This was kind of an interesting AP for me.

I was completely naked and gravity was heavy. Around me were the shambles of my neighborhood. The houses (what was left of them) were falling down and deteriorating. There were no more lawns or grass just piles and heaps of dirt. I could feel the grit between my toes. I was quickly losing the small amount of rationality I had left and slipping into a nightmare.

Suddenly a group of soldiers come over a hill. There were about 10 of them and they were wearing modern military fatigues with the American flag emblazoned on their left shoulder. On their right shoulder was what looked like a pyramid with an eye inside it.

They surrounded me and I felt really awkward being all naked and dirty. The leader started asking me things like, "what are you doing out here?" and "what could you possibly be looking for out here? You know where you are? John do a scan on him." So "John" gets behind me and puts one hand under my chin and the other on top of my head. "Just relax. Just relax." I stay still until John says to his leader, "He's an innocent!" They get into some discussion about me. I guess they are surprised to find an "innocent" this far out here. "Well someone has to take him back."

They are a little frustrated that they have to deal with me at this point but a truck appears out of nowhere and they tell me to get inside. I get in the front with the driver on one side and another soldier on my right. We start driving so fast down a road and I get a good view of all the damage.

I start to see familiar places from environments from dreams I had like 6 months ago. We go farther and farther and now I'm seeing things from dreams I had years ago. The truck is going through barricades without stopping. Things look nice again and there's pretty trees and neighborhoods again. Finally we stop at a train station that looks pretty clean and modern. The soldiers let me out of the truck and one of them says to me in parting, "Take care now. Don't go too far next time ok?" Without a second glance they ride off.

I wake up soon after that. That's like the second time I've had someone take me "back" when I was lost. Maybe it's not such a good idea to get lost out there huh?

Switching Minds

February 14, 2021

Last night was probably one of the strangest lucid dreams I've had. At first I found myself fishing for huge fish from this rocky beach. There where a few other people fishing for big game there too. For some reason every time you caught one of these big fish you had to be careful how you reeled it in or you ended up with a fish with a broken neck. I finally got a bite and reeled in my fish through the shoals without a broken neck.

The next part was about an old lady and some kind of teacher. The teacher was explaining how we would switch minds me and this old lady. It was supposed to teach us what it's like being other people. Well, the teacher did his magic and I was suddenly inside the body of an old lady. But the thing is the body came with the brain or mind of the person too. It was super awkward at first trying to understand what was happening. The teacher explained that we would not only have the body of this new person but the mind and feelings as well. Well... like I said, it was super weird. I had to learn to walk in a new body but also how she felt walking. I had all these new feelings I can't even describe.

The old lady had my body and mind and it was strange seeing myself move around as someone else. As I settled into it I realized all these pressing "weights" on my new mind. I realized they were worries. The old lady had three children and I realized I worried a lot about them. My husband was dead and I missed him terribly. I was worried about money too and what I would do if I got evicted.

Well after about 30 minutes the teacher returned to separate us and put us back into our own body and minds. I had been visiting with my three new children who I loved so much. The teacher did his magic and I felt a sudden relief to be myself again. It felt like taking a dip in a nice warm and familiar bath. It felt so good to be back.

The next part was me and this old lady talking about our experiences to each other and going around to other couples and seeing how they were doing. Many people where experiencing switching bodies and minds. I didn't really bother them it was just like watching a movie. I learned a lot from watching other people switch minds and bodies too. There was this couple who switched and the wife had found out some real secrets about him - like how he had left a family behind in his younger years and how bad he felt about it.

Virtual Room

February 19, 2021

I was so tired but decided to try exiting anyway. When I had reached my level, I separated. I found myself in very different surroundings.

I was laying in bed in what looked like a college dorm room. There was another bed on the opposite wall and a desk next to each bed. Everything looked pristine and beautiful and fresh with sparkle. I got out of bed and found the door. The door wouldn't open until I hit a blue lighted button next to it. It slid sideways like a Star Trek door.

Outside was a long hallway which I followed for a long time in silence. It came to a beautiful garden area which had many paths veering at right angles. This is when I started seeing all these panels with techy displays with buttons. They were in the walls of every corner. It felt like this place had a form of virtualization. I went up to one of the big displays in the middle of the gardens and saw a map of the levels. One said "Store" so I went there by hitting it on the panel. I was immediately outside the Store which looked like a modern mall but with many more plants and brightness. I went in.

I wandered around and it looked like a regular store with tons of stuff to buy. Before I can see what's for sale I bump into one of the clerks which asks, "Is there anything I can help you find?" I try to speak but my voice cracks and I can't speak right for some reason. The clerk brings out some device and a window in space appears with text and icon boxes. "You're missing most of the base add-ons but you have one very interesting add-on. This icon represents a free soul," he explained. The icon showed a tree with three big leaves. We went around the store adding "add-ons" to my inventory. By the end I could talk like normal and float.

I remember going back to my room but I found 6 people there going through my things. I got the hang of the techy panels and dialed myself a new private room. It was nice and cozy in darkness with blue, red, and yellows. Colored crystals hung from the ceiling and the dim lighting revealed a nice plush chair with entertainment system. Off to one side is a nice big bed in dark blue. On one wall is a desk with a panel. I can't really explain but there was this feeling of safety that felt so good.

I went to sleep on the bed and got some real good sleep.

Energy Snake

March 5, 2021

I had prayed for a vision of Light for about a week. Last night I finally got it.

I don't remember how I exited my body but when I became lucid I was in this garden waiting outside an office of sorts to see someone. It was almost like it had been scripted and I was playing a part. Suddenly this nice old man came out and said "Come in Sergio! We've been waiting for you." I went into his office, a nice brick little building in the midst of this amazing garden, and he sat me down. He explained that he was the head of this school and gifted children of Light come here to be tested. I said OK to most of what he was talking about until he got to the part about the Test. I inquired, "What kind of test is it?" He explained that it was a test to see how well I could handle the Life Stream. He said that every gifted child of Light has some knack in handling it and he wanted to see what area I was using.

He shuffled me out of the door and I was guided by a woman in a robe who took me to this big Old Tree. The tree was enormous and there was a door in it. Around me were all kinds of other people. As I waited to be let into the Tree I had a conversation with a few other initiates who had already taken the Test. They chatted my ear off about all this amazing stuff that had happened to them while they handled the Life Stream. I was more than a little excited to see what I could do with it.

The old man who had seen to me earlier finally arrived and he opened the door to this big beautiful Tree and let me in. Inside where all kinds of flashing lights dancing in fractal patterns. There where mists that went on forever and chasms of Light. The old man explained a few things to me. He said that as the Life Stream flowed through me I would naturally know what to do with it. He said not to worry and gave me a few telepathic visions of what other people could do with it. I was quite blown away with all the abstractions of Light that poured into my head. He closed the door behind him and I was left alone in this big room of Light.

Suddenly I was charged with Life. It was like a giant python of Light had been put in my hands and it was my job to steer it and control it... but it wasn't in my hands - it flowed through my very soul. It was so much Power all at once! It roared like a thousand lions! I "grabbed" unto it and I just was There! I was in that area where you can go only alone. It was so powerful! It was like I was a filament of Light itself. And I surfed this million-gigawatt beam of Light and pointed it straight to the Heavens where I climbed and soared higher and higher.

The vision only lasted about a minute. Then I was gently placed on the ground and the Light dimmed down slowly... and then I was alone.

Turning Into a Woman

March 14, 2021

I went to sleep kind of late. I notice that the later I stay up the more intense my APs are. After a slow clumsy separation I found myself in a beautiful castle room with pink drapes and soft blue hues. Around me were girls. Tons of them! They had me surrounded!

A few took me in hand and led me to an old style bathtub where they proceeded to wash me thoroughly. After that they dyed my hair raven black. After that I got a manicure and a pedicure. Looking in a mirror I could see that my black hair was long now like a girl.

Here comes the weird part. Naked as I was the girls surrounded me again and a few came forth to stimulate me. Once I was erect a beautiful blond came forth with a beautiful sword and with one swing chopped it off! I screamed! Another girl came forth and carved what was left of my manhood out! Looking down I could see a gaping slit with blood where my pee-pee used to be!

"It's almost over! Don't worry!" one of the pretty girls was saying. One girl had a device which she then scanned me with a blue light on my parts. Suddenly I had a full blown vagina. As far as vaginas go I thought it was pretty decent! They did their scan again and suddenly I had breasts!

Well, they dressed me up in a nice dress and put me in front of this regal mirror. I was a beautiful girl!

Party House

March 25, 2021

I went to sleep exhausted. I got in bed and fell asleep. I woke back up in a few minutes though but then realized I was in the astral. I was still in bed though so I got up and ran outside.

Everything was dark outside except for one house down the street that was very well lighted. I floated and zipped down the street. There were many people at the house. Most were talking together or just walking around or I saw some people having a beer and smoking. I went into the house to explore the party.

There was a couch inside in the living room and there was this pretty girl sitting on it. She was reading a thick book. I sat down and wanted to talk to her but she seemed very concentrated with her book. I started playing with her hair and she looked up to me. I said hi and asked her if I could have a kiss. She smiled and I kissed her. She kissed me back and we did that for a while. After that I went back outside.

Something was going on outside. People had gathered to watch an art of war. Two boys where manipulating reality and making dream manifestations. They used lines that created the shape and then gave it life. The two dream shapes were kind of fighting each other like an astral version of a wrestling match. The two crazy shapes had all kind of ingenious shapes to fight each other. They came together and tried to dominate the other. The two boys responsible had their arms out into the sky as they brought their line shapes to life.

Finally, they shapes turned into spaceships and the two boys took to the air as they rode them. They fought in mid-air and came crashing down unto the ground. In the middle of this spaghetti mess of lines the two boys came together and started playing another game. I couldn't follow it fully but it was some kind of intellect game trading lines together and seeing who could fool who.

Anyway, that's when I went home. Went down the street and found my house. I went in and back to my bed. It was empty and I fell into it and woke up. I had been out for about 50 minutes. I went back to sleep and awoke the next day after considerably more vivid dreams than I usually have.

Heaven and Hell

April 5, 2021

Last night was the second time I've had an experience like this. I was lucid but I was kind of a different person. I was still me but I was also another version of myself.

This version of myself was a spiritual warrior who had relocated to the Badlands to study evil. Not to practice it of course, but to gain knowledge of it so I could defeat it.

This time I had built a little hut on the lower hell realms and I was studying this group of hell beings incognito. I had a magic bubble that disguised me and helped hide me. I was watching these hell beings with my binoculars from about 25 meters away. They were some kind of organized sect that practiced evil. They where going through some ritual dances as I watched them. On their faces they had living worms and their flesh looked bruised and rotten. They chanted and swung big knives around.

I could feel the environment around me. The bad vibes were palpable this close to the hell realms. I reminded myself that the information I gathered here was valuable and would help me in the War. The only war. The war against the dark side...

I was watching these beings and suddenly one of them saw me or sensed me. He yelled and all of them got really excited. They spotted me and started running in my direction. I panicked and started running toward Heaven. Somehow I knew in which direction to go and I ran for all my life. I could hear screams of anger coming closer behind me.

I ran and ran away from hell. I passed forgotten ruins and slowed down. They where really pretty and I found myself in a beautiful enchanted forest. The ruins where scattered through it. I forgot about the hell beings knowing I had left them behind. Everything was so quiet except for the caw of a raven somewhere in the trees. I came to this open area where sunlight beams where streaking from above. Dust motes hung in the air and one small little moth flapped its wings above me. The moth was making the most beautiful little sounds like a flute. There was a thin quiet high frequency sound like the type a crystal might make when it's vibrated with electricity.

I kept on walking and entered a long lit hallway. It came to a ballroom with a grand staircase that went up to the higher realms. There where people there and singularities of light. But for some reason I couldn't move as fast. The closer I got to the staircase the slower I moved. I noticed that everyone close to the top was moving very slowly. It didn't feel like I was being impeded but that I was entering a different realm. One were reverence was needed and a much slower more appreciative awareness.

I kept on moving forward and with it came patience and stillness and a sense of wholesomeness. I inched my way up the stairs and into the Light. Amen.

<u>Money</u>

April 12, 2021

I find it interesting the concept of money in the astral. Some astral planes use currency but some don't. I personally have always been able to pay for stuff that is on sale. I've been to a few astral bazzars and they use a credit based system with astral tech. When I use my astral wallet there's always money in it. So I don't understand if everyone is dreaming of money and it's not real or maybe the currency is valid within the astral plane.

I remember one time I landed on an astral plane with thieves and rip-off artists. They would go around in groups ripping people off of their wallet money. After I got ripped off I found my wallet brimming with money... so it sounds like they are just dreaming of ripping people off instead of really ripping people off. I personally think money is pointless in the astral. Maybe it's just a leftover affectation from physical world based currency.

Astral Dream Clouds

April 18, 2021

I went to sleep very tired but still had some giddy energy so it took me awhile to fall asleep. I had programmed myself for an exit and when I became lucid I floated/hopped out of bed and went into the night. I was expecting it to be dark outside in the astral but I was shocked to see the whole neighborhood all lighted up despite the darkness of the night. It was as if the houses had been painted with neon or phosphorescent paint. They looked so colorful and pretty.

I started by floating down the street and taking a good look at my neighborhood. It was beautiful with all the special colors. I decided to go into one of the houses as they sometimes serve as gateways into further astral explorations. I chose a charming house done in white and blue. In I went. The door was unlocked as usual.

Inside it was also well lighted and it looked pretty normal and clean. The light wasn't coming from a source. Like I said, everything seemed phosphorescent. On one wall was a big mirror. As I stared at it it changed and became a tunnel. It was super cool and so I crept into the mirror and found myself inside an underground tunnel. The tunnel was made of stone with all kinds of angles. I negotiated my way around turns and dips and finally found an exit to the surface. What greeted me was out of this world.

I was in the clouds. It was super bright. It was abstract. In the clouds were pictures like a comic book - very detailed pictures that moved like animations. As I inspected the animations I realized they where scenes from some of my favorite shows on TV like Game of Thrones! I went closer to one cloud with a dragon in it. I went into the cloud and suddenly I was just there riding the dragon through vast landscapes. He was gorgeous and while I rode my dragon new clouds appeared that gave me all kinds of new possibilities. In one cloud I could land in a castle and make love to the dragon queen herself. In another I could lead a team of dragon riders against the zombie dead. It was so cool!

I must have spent hours going from dream cloud to dream cloud. I wish I could remember it all. I really enjoyed myself with this one. Wish I could describe it better but words just don't suffice to make this type of astral experience well... describable! I was so out there! I hope heaven is like this and if it was I would not be disappointed.

The Nuevo Family

April 22, 2021

This was a really detailed lucid dream. I can't really figure out why I had it but it was truly fascinating.

This is the story of the Nuevo Family. They live in the 23rd century where Greg Nuevo, the father, is a great inventor and quantum field specialist. He was the guy that advanced quantum fields like antigravity, shields, and tractor beams. He became especially famous for inventing the quantum egg which is a personal shield and transportation device that fits over a human body.

Well, Greg was also a very enlightened dude and in his mid-thirties he and his wife Laura put up many meditation centers. These became very popular because they were extremely beautiful meditation centers at one with Nature. Greg and Laura had started what was to be called the Egg Transcendence.

Later, Greg became even more famous when he developed a system for nudging avalanches before they could collapse and reek havoc. He used his field technology to trigger the avalanches in a controlled fashion. He could be seen inside his quantum egg driving the avalanche down off the mountain. It was a spectacular site. The headline read: "Greg Nuevo Drives the World."

After that the Nuevos had two children. I was introduced to their teenage daughter who took me on my first tour to Greg's new invention, the quantum tunnels. There where tunnels like in a water park but instead of water they used quantum fields and brain scanning technology. You could ride a tunnel and create amazing firestorms of plasma inside them by imagining them. My trip down a tunnel was amazing and Sara Nuevo, Greg's first daughter, showed me a firestorm she had made down one of the large tunnels. It was beautiful... we rode the tunnel as fields of red and violet plasma danced around us.

Well, Greg's last and final invention was really a doozy and quite controversial. He built a giant quantum bubble city. The thing was that the bubble flipped (inverted) as thousands of his followers entered the field. They just vanished! All they left was a spectacular miasma of energy that could be seen by touring the city from the inside. Some said they had died a spectacular death but it was theorized that the people who had been inverted continued on in a new form of Life. Yep, you guessed it... that was how Greg and Laura "died"... they were inverted when the bubble city flipped.

The Nuevo children went on to have children of their own and many still live in the bubble city giving tours and running the meditation centers. How about those Nuevos?

Game Cartridges

May 2, 2021

This one was more than an astral projection, it was a vision. I woke up suddenly. I was falling into churning brown river water and then I was being pulled with the current downriver. I managed to grab unto an edge and found cold obsidian. I nevertheless pulled myself unto the land. Everywhere were sharp edges and it was impossible to walk without cutting your feet. I decided to plunge back in the water and see what was downriver.

I was taken downriver and I find a small alcove set next to a cliff. No sharp edges. Nice soft brown dirt. It's a small place but cozy. In one corner is an open newspaper like someone has been reading. In the middle are 25 different game cartridges still in their wrappers. Only one game cartridge is open and only the wrapper remains - it says Sergio46.

I saw myself Reading that newspaper and being myself - flashing through to another side that was a separate reality. And I thought about those other games in the packages. And I wondered what they were...

Apple Melons

May 24, 2021

Suddenly, I was lucid and sitting in an arm chair staring at keleidoscope patterns in a fireplace. It was the picture of cozy. It looked like the most comfortable wooden cabin. I went outside and saw that my cabin was one of eight. There was a dirt road with four cabins on either side. Around this little village was a deep forest with tall healthy trees.

I saw someone come out of the cabin across the street and we started talking. He was a young man around my age and he was very friendly. We instantly became buddies. A man and woman were approaching the cabin next to mine. They were each carrying a sack full of something. My new friend asked them what they were carrying and the guy said, "apple melons."

Suddenly there was a low rumble like far-away thunder. We all looked toward the horizon and could see a big storm coming. And I mean a big storm - the clouds where almost black.

"Get inside! Get inside! Sergio has the strongest house so we'll all meet there. Get your apple melons everyone and bring them to Sergio's." Everyone went to get their apple melons. I helped my neighbor carry a few sacks to my house. I was almost to my door when the entire sky turned black and the wind started howling. I could hear crazy haunting voices in the deep dark fog. And then there was darkness. I used my flashlight to find my house. My neighbors followed me in carrying the last of the apple melons. We closed and bolted the door.

Outside you could hear the storm howling. The best part of the dream happened next. My neighbor took a small box from his belt and said, "PROTECT!" then he threw the small cube at the windows. The little box expanded and the two Guardians stepped out. They looked like super cool characters from a comic book or something. One had huge muscles and looked like a Viking warrior. The other had a mane of spikes around and on his head that made him look like a sun god. They did a little dance and then merged into the windows making sort of a barrier.

We hunkered down and waited for the storm to pass. This was obviously no ordinary storm. I could hear crazy laughter coming from outside and the windows and doors rattled noisily. It was pretty scary.

Something bumped into my leg and a looked down to see the cutest white kitten. I sat down and petted the little cat which purred and butted his head against my hand.

"Here Sergio," someone said. I looked up and someone had cut and peeled some apple melons on a plate. I took a piece and put it in my mouth. It tasted like apples and watermelons!

Jack the Rat

June 3, 2021

I keep finding new ways to exit. This time I was dozing and I started to imagine myself running in a forest. Slowly the trees got more vivid and background music started to play. I can't imagine who was playing such beautiful music. I glided up into the sky and saw towns and beautiful neighborhoods. The people seemed so real. I landed in the second story of a bar.

Inside was a group of people who I talked to. The first talk was about how getting close to the center of the universe dissolved you into pure Spirit. Someone said they where 47% sure they could go all the way soon and become pure Spirit.

Then Jack the Rat showed up and said he would tell my prophecy. He said you can tell how old a soul is by the amount of times it had touched the Truth. He said I had touched it at least once in my current life and I would touch it again before it was over. I woke up right after that.

Astral Suit

July 20, 2021

I detached from my body easily and struggled up to a standing position (I had been sleeping in my bean bag). In front of me was the most amazing astral suit! It looked like a space suit with helmet. I knew instinctively what to do and put it on. Somehow my astral knowledge was working again and I knew I was in luck! I donned the suit on and immediately felt the extra strength and abilities. I headed out of my room and outside. I opened my front door and was greeted by a nighttime neighborhood. My street was all dark except way down where I could see a well lighted building. I immediately set course. With my new suit it took me less than 5 seconds. Everything was so easy... it knew exactly what I wanted.

The building was luxurious with pink and yellow lights and a few trees in the front yard. I went inside. Inside where offices and what looked like lab rooms all behind glass walls. A woman with dark long straight hair saw me and came out of one of the rooms.

"So how do you like the new suit?" I told her it was very comfortable and very fast plus it makes me super lite. I asked if I could take a tour of the factory and she called over one of the head developers who took me through the building. Toward the back he showed me the next astral suit model they weere working on. He pushed a button and this pod opened from the wall and the suit came out. I asked him how it all worked. He told me the inputs where pretty much direct - sun to sun, moon to moon... some stuff was beyond me.

"Ready for a higher elevation? Just press that button." I pressed an orange button on my suit's arm band and I was suddenly in another place. Well... it looked like an astral center. I was inside a building like a big mall but it was pleasing. It had like 10 levels. I floated down to the center floor where a nice garden was evident. Someone was sitting there next to a large display. As I passed him he spoke up to me and said, "Come back... and stand right there." There was some kind of astral camera pointed at me. As it captured my image the large display showed a giant modern complex surrounded by forests. It was pretty... and there was a giant four-legged robot protecting the complex. "Interesting," the guy said, "looks like you might be a 67."

I floated up to level 6 and walked down one of the long hallways. I saw a lot of astral stores. I saw a lady with a helmet on and some guy guiding her with some kind of goggles on his head. Maybe some kind of new hypnosis? I went into the next room which had a picture of a woman smelling a flower.

Inside was another man. "Sit down, sit down," he said. I sat next to him and suddenly I smelled the most beautiful smell I have ever smelled. It was like flowers and wild jasmine. "Wow, you smell good." I asked if that was my astral scent and he concurred. I could also smell a cigar smell but it was coming from the guy. "And that's your smell?" I asked. "Afraid so... I smoke cigars and it gets into everything. Even the astral body."

I wandered around the astral mall. It wasn't crowded at all, just a few people. I heard two people talking about food pills down on level 2. One said she had tried the KFC pill and it had overloaded her taste with yummy KFC chicken. "It was so good!"

Observations #3

August 1, 2021

I think there's something strange about the astral. The more time I hang out there the stranger I feel. It really is like an alien planet or a parallel dimension. Whenever I go deep I always come back with the strangest taste in my mouth - almost like my energy is vibrating at a different frequency than Earth does. It takes a few hours sometimes to get that feel off me. It's weird anyway.

Then, it's the people I meet in my travels. Some are just plain spooks. Been dead for so long they've camped out at some place out there and some aren't so pretty. Then there are the shiny people who have real nice healthy glows and attitudes. I can at least hang out with them and have a conversation. If it's a pretty girl it can get better real quick if you know how to charm them. Everyone's a lot more honest in the astral. If there's a connection it's quickly obvious. Probably it's because we're closer to our essential natures. So you say and do what you want and it comes out beautiful.

Then there are the Guardians, helpers, and collaborators. They are always around. They keep tabs on all their sheep. I know I have a few taking care of me. You just have to keep making inroads toward the Light and you'll find them. Never known them to be anything but helpful and friendly although sometimes a little distant like there's some professionalism about it. But they deal in Love and have instant and huge access to its essence. I got a Love shower once and it felt like it was raining pure laughter and happiness.

Then there are the scouts. Those are beings sent out from some place in the infinite astral to lure visitors to their domain. They're not that common but I've bumbed into them from time to time. They took me to really wild and strange places I never could of dreamed of.

It's so cool to be able to explore whole new worlds. There's so much to see and learn.

<u>Moving Day</u>

August 5, 2021

Last night was really trippy. At some point I found myself lucid, traveling down a deserted dirt road with one male and two attractive females.

"Feel like making some headway?" asked one of the girls with flowers in her hair. I said I would and that I would protect her while on the journey. I wondered at my words. Some part of me knew exactly what was going on. I could tell she was the leader of our foursome. She smiled and kissed me passionately on the lips. I could tell this girl was a young goddess and that she and her friends were running from something or someone.

The male companion belonged to the other girl among us and together we traveled down the road with hippy back-packs on our backs. I wondered what personality persuasion had attracted me to this group. I began to ask my girl some questions as to what our journey was about.

"It's moving day again. You know how it is... we have to stay ahead of the meanies. Common Sergio, you remember," she said. I remembered then... yeah it was moving day. I looked down the road which we had traveled about a mile and could tell that it was darker behind us and brighter in front of us with a promise of hope.

More than anything I wanted to stop and have some time with my girl who kept her head down and kept striding forward. She was one of the most beautiful girls I have ever seen. The more I thought of her the more I remembered. We had done this many times before. This same group, these same people. They were my "moving" group and perhaps the only thing that had kept us together was our destination. We were headed towards the Light looking for schools along the way where we could stop and learn the ways of love and light.

We stopped after a while and brought out some fruit from our back-packs. It was juicy as I fed a guava looking fruit to my girlfriend. She took a big bite and smied, juice runing down her face. We talked and I kissed her again passionately. She smiled and said, "Not here."

A bird was signing down to us. We all looked up. It wasn't a bird it was a magic moth. A big one. It was absolutely beautiful with big haunting eyes on it's wings.

"It's time to keep moving," said she and got up from the cozy grass. We packed up our belongings and were back on the road with our moth showing the way Home.

Plush

August 10, 2021

I noticed I was lucid and asleep so I performed an exit. At this point I was deep enough into the trance to leave no body behind - I just got up and went outside. It was nighttime like in the real world. I could see stars and some puffy clouds. I saw a house with a light on and headed toward it. It was kind of far away so I tried to fly there. I went too high however and I got lost in the sky. It was dark and I went into limbo for a second. Then I saw a cross on the ground. It was made of lights. I noticed it was the lights of an airport.

I could now see passenger jets and I remembered that there was indeed an airport nearby. I landed and explored the airport which was full of people. I quickly got out of there and tried to fly back to my neighborhood. I landed in a dark street with a few lights on. I chose the nearest house with a light and went in. Inside were four people sitting around in the living room. One was a really pretty girl so I went up to her and asked, "You want to show me your room?" She knew instantly what I was talking about and took my hand and stood up.

Hand in hand she led me toward the back of the house where she stopped at a blank wall and started touching the wall at the level where there should be a knob. Suddenly there was a knob. Suddenly there was a door and she opened it and we went inside.

Inside was a small room. It was so cozy like a little nook full of trinkets. In the adjoining room was a round plush bed with a fur blanket. We started kissing then and she tasted normally - maybe even a little sweet. Sometimes you get an awful taste and that sort of warns you off some astral women.

This girl was sweet and warm and loving. It felt really good to be with someone astral healthy.

I had a fun night... I've decided that you can't really delete the sexual aspect of the universe. It happens and it just opens up another way to learn and love.

Authorities

August 21, 2021

Something interesting happened the last two nights. I got out of body and went outside. It was daytime and my sidewalk looked like a busy street. There were lots people walking back and forth. This is the first time though I spotted an authority. There were two of them and they had uniforms and looked exactly like security. I went right by them and they looked friendly but attentive to all that was going on.

Then last night I AP again and it's night time and the whole street has security cars with their lights on. I tried to see what was going on and saw like this security team pulling this dark cloud of fuzzy energy out of a house. There were three men in black pushing this cloud into a van. I must of woken right after I saw that.

I wonder what that was all about?

Astral House

August 28, 2021

Last night was an amazing astral projection. I found myself lucid in the most beautiful house I have ever lived in. I knew I was in the astral or some type of Heaven because everything looked so beautiful. The colors and things just stood out and the spaces themselves almost shone with light.

I found myself in this dream or AP and the astral voice told me that this is where I would most likely spend my time after death. I prayed to God right then and there if I could just stay here now and forever - that I didn't have to go back to Earth. It didn't work because I am typing this message but the house was so beautiful that I never wanted to leave. My room was gigantic and had two levels. The house itself had about 6 stories to it. My Mom and Dad lived there with me too. As I explored the house I saw that they were having a party along with all the neighbors. They all came over and gave me big genuine hugs and I felt so loved. I really wonder where this magical house is? Things I wanted seemed to appear out of nowhere just for my convenience. Toys, candy, games. It was truly a modern magical house.

I must of spent hours in my house just playing and wandering around. Almost like rediscovering my old place of venue. Not a dull moment went by. The second I was done doing something, something just as marvelous would present itself. It was truly a nexus, a real Heaven.

After exploring my house which seemed oddly familiar to me... I went and found my Mom. I explained to her that I have this life far, far, away in another planet called Earth. For the first time things started going awry. She got mad and said "We don't talk about those things darling." And then she seemed to go back to her own LaLa world.

I never wanted to leave. But eventually I found myself back in my bed on old planet Earth. How real it had seemed and familiar. Almost like at this very moment I am there with my magical family in my magical house. I can see where the term multi-dimensional might be used. I exist there in my own Heaven but for now... I also exist here on Earth. I can't wait to go back to my House though!

Multiverse Starship

September 1, 2021

Last night I had one of those super lucid dreams. I was myself but at the same time I was my dreamer self. I can see that they are different - there's the small me and the big super dreamer me. They are both I but my dreamer knows crazy things about the universe. Things my little me finds hard to understand. Both sides are the self but they are like two modes to my soul.

Last night I was both of them. I dreamed that Levar Burton (Geordi on Star Trek) came to me and asked if I could spearhead a new Star Trek show with him. My dreamer-self told him he had a great idea about a child who was the Sun. Whatever happened to this child happened to the Sun. And whatever happened to the Sun happened to the child. The boy was the Sun and the Sun was the boy. But something went wrong and Geordi said he wouldn't help in making that kind of show because if there was a Sun child it would mean the boy was special and that made him jealous.

Then something happened and I was granted the funding by a higher source to create this new Star Trek show.

The next part was me putting this Star Trek show together. I picked a crew and I created their spaceship. The spaceship's bridge was a quarter mile square of aqua blue pool of water like a lagoon. There were these spikes of water in the pool that each held an orb at its point. They moved in crazy patterns. Up above on a cliff was the center of the bridge where the controls where input by the crew. Looked like the control center at NASA just super modern with jazzed up displays.

We started shooting the first show and in this one we explored the big bridge which would take our ship otherworld into the multiverses. It was super neat exploring this new bridge type. The order was there and it seems so crazy to my ordinary mind.

It ended by someone falling off a cliff and needing to be taken to the infirmary. The bridge of our othership could be hazardous to explore. So the crew learned that they had to be careful.

Spiderweb Jacuzzi

September 17, 2021

I've been having some trouble exiting lately. I would get out of body but would jolt back to my body after a few seconds. This happened for like three nights in a row. Finally last night I had a clean exit.

I exited my body after watching myself fall asleep. When I could move my astral body I separated. I did not exit in my regular room. It was my old room at my old house. It was so weird seeing my old room and house. I went out of the room and went outside. It was snowing just like those beautiful Michigan winters I remember. I crossed the road and went across the street to a house to see if I could find something interesting.

The door to the house was open so I went inside. Inside was a living room and toward the back was a spiral staircase that went up and up and up. I followed it all the way up until at the top it ended in a little nook that had cushions and a large television. I sat down to watch tv and they were showing a hotel ad for this really luxurious hotel. I got really into it because this hotel was gorgeous. They showed the main entrance and suddenly it was me going into the hotel and I was walking into the main lobby.

I was greeted like a special guest by this pretty girl in uniform and given a key, then escorted to my room. I remember exploring my room and it was beautiful. I then took the elevator to the floor where they had a pool and sauna. The pool was cool but at the back they had this really special jacuzzi. It was on an elevated pedestal and instead of water it had a liquid with these dark spiderweb patterns in it. I was curious so I got in.

The spiderwebs sort of latched unto my body and it felt amazing! I started having these amazing states of consciousness I can hardly describe. It was like a consciousness entertainment system. I must of spent awhile going from state to state until I heard someone say, "Hey, it's my turn! You've been in there long enough." I saw some girl standing there so I got out and went back to my room. I think I woke up soon after that. What a cool jacuzzi!

Dark House

September 23, 2021

Last night I APed and it was a little scary. I exited and went outside like normal. Usually there are lights on at least one house but this time the whole street was dark. I flew up into the air to get a better view and the whole neighborhood was dark. I landed and took stock. What would happen if I went into a dark house? Huh.

I landed and approached the nearest house across the street. I was going to explore a dark house. I reached for the knob of the front door and opened it. Right in front of me is this girl dressed in pajamas and she looks at me with this far off look. I kissed her on the cheek and instantly woke up.

Beach House

October 1, 2021

This was a AP at the beach. I must have been walking down the white sandy beach when I see someone walking toward me. The moment I recognized him I became fully lucid. It was my dead father of 6 years now. He gave me a huge hug and asked me how I was doing. I told him I really missed him and that it's been awhile since I last seen him. He motioned me in a direction away from the ocean toward this big house on the beach. He looked like he was 30 years younger - healthy.

As we were walking toward his house some people were coming out of the ocean on a small fishing boat. My Dad goes over to them and asks, "Did you catch anything?"

"Sure thing!" says a woman and we look inside the boat and here is a giant tuna fish. My father offers to cook it up for them and so we make our way toward the beach house which is really a restaurant. My Dad's dream was to run a restaurant. He used to run one when he was alive for a while.

So I check out the house/restaurant and there are living quarters on top of the restaurant. One of the rooms is my own room from my old house. It was like I was home except my house had been converted to a beach house. I hear my Dad calling from downstairs so I go down and he's serving everyone some cooked up fish with rice and salad. He hands me a plate and I go sit down at a booth. This girl sits down right after me with her plate. I ask her name and she says Vanessa Cole. Then she smiles and says, "Vanessa Cool."

The food was delicious and I got to see my Dad one more time to say goodbye. I gave him a big hug and told him not to be a stranger. I also remember saying that I was so glad he was doing so well.

It was cool to see my Dad again. I just hope the astral is really like that and we get to spend our time with the people we love.

Astral School

October 11, 2021

Last night was interesting. It was another of those dreams where I'm lucid but my super dreamer at the same time. After exiting into my room I knew I had a tour at one of the astral schools. I went outside and take the bus which was waiting for me to the school. I know exactly all the spots which are on my list and so I spend my time visiting the campus which were a series of buildings throughout this beautiful city.

The streets where sunny and had lots of trees. I would stop at a building and some force would guide me yet I never heard a voice. I greeted other students in the middle of their projects. They looked super busy but were kind enough to explain what specific task they were working on. To me, now awake, it seemed they were doing something like creating software or videogames but with the astral - trying to crack some algorithm or something.

The whole ordeal ended by me signing up for some astral classes at Admissions.

Heaven or Hell?

November 7, 2021

I dreamt of a place where you are drawn to whenever you want to go into the astral and have fun. It's called the Crossroads and there are heavenly games and darker more dangerous games. I wandered around and decided whether to go see the Heaven games or the darker games... games that were made for darker aspects.

I found some interesting games "below". One, they try to rip off your energy by showing you the grossest astral images. It was like a haunted house ride where they really want to suck your blood. I allowed it to develop because I wanted to learn something new. Even as I was being tricked into leaking a pint of energy or two, I knew I had to experience it to see if it was real. Whatever was on that ride was gross but was supposed to feel super good. The scary thing is I think it does work on some level to the untrained and undisciplined mind. Most was super sexual and other stuff was just gross. All the while there's some vampire process going on as you go.

Anyway, I got out of there and tried to find a higher more Heavenly plane. For me, I just can't believe people actually could do that... create these terrible games in the astral where they try to take your vital forces. Remind me never to go there again.

I entered Heaven and saw that they were giving away Tolkien chocolates in one street corner. I ate two and dreamt I was with Gandalf.

Antivirus 2714

November 16, 2021

I had a lucid dream where I was the head of a big software company. We were in a meeting when "Linda" runs in and screams: "We've been hacked! All the servers are going down!" We all rush out of the meeting room and I head to my office. On my computer screen I can see the virus taking over our computers. It hits the main server and I start feeling dizzy and then my limbs won't work and I go down. At the same time there is this guy in my head laughing and laughing.

The next thing I see is this old wooden printer. It was like a modern computer printer but all stylized and made of wood. There is a long roll of paper coming out of it with stylized fonts. The camera zooms in and it's a list of names - dead people names. One of the names is mine. I see it come out of the printer and roll down as more names are printed out. It was very eerie especially because in the background is this sound. The sound is of a panting woman rushing down some stairs in high heels. You can tell she is running from something and she is scared and all you hear is the clop-clop of her high-heeled shoes in panic going down risky steps in a run.

I catch a last look at my name before it fades into darkness as the paper disappears into oblivion. Just before it disappears I see a hand of someone with white sleeves reach out and grab the name with his fingers. It comes off the paper like a sticker.

The next thing I know, I am waking up back into the dream where I am at my software company. I have no control of my body. I am just the eyes looking out. I see myself get up and my body goes over to my desk and opens up a file cabinet. There are some disks there and one is labeled "Antivirus 2714". I see myself put in the disk into the drive and I open up a window and execute a file. Suddenly I see this graphic of my servers coming back online. The whole system is restored and suddenly I'm back in my body.

Linda walks into my office and says, "We're back up! What did you do??" I say, "I just used my Antivirus 2714."

Goddess

December 2, 2021

Last night I was easily able to separate from the physical. I entered a trance right after falling asleep and exited cleanly. As usual, I went outside and behold! There is a river flowing down the street and the day looks muggy. I see my ex-girlfriend flow down the river and I see she's in trouble trying to keep her head above water. I have to decide for a while and then something takes over and I'm in the water going after her.

Somehow I catch up with her and our presence together seems to calm the river down and we look at each other mystified. Then she has this green light flash her and she stars rising out of the water. She walks on the water and makes it to land. I follow after her easily making my way out. Together we take off to the hills.

We cross a desert to a town of a few people. My ex-girlfriend has all of them enchanted and awestruck with her beauty. Indeed she was a Goddess which I had stumbled upon. I gave her room to expand with my powers protecting her and keeping her safe. In return she would give me a kiss which was the sweetest nectar of passion that I knew only true Love could surpass. But this she kept from me and her secret heart flew to the Unknowns.

We made it to the big city where she was the talk of the town. Soon they crowned her their new queen and somehow... I was king.

I woke up refreshed knowing I had seen the Goddess inside my girlfriend. I was awestruck at her beauty.

Hug

December 8, 2021

Last night I had an interesting dream I want to write down. It was about an Indian family from India. There was a father, a mother, and a single son. I felt I was playing the part of the son because as the story was being told I could feel his emotions.

Well, we weren't the richest family. We rented a small apartment and didn't have a car. But we were very religious and austere. Our religion was what kept our little family together. It's also what kept us apart. The son loved his parents very much but for some reason their religion got in the way of hugging and kissing and signs of affection. It really made him sad that he couldn't express these feelings. I think it was the father who kept it that way because of his religion.

Anyway, years went by and I grew up (the son) and my parents separated and I was going to go to school on my own for the first time. I was at the bus station with my father and it was so painful. The boy wanted to hug his father goodbye but it "wasn't allowed". We said goodbye and didn't even shake hands and this left me feeling so lonely.

At the end of the dream… the boy stops going to school and makes a visit to his mother who is a teacher of archeology at this point. He cries and cries as he finally allows himself to give his mother a hug.

I don't know why I had this dream. Me and my family are very affectionate. We hug all the time. Maybe it was a past life or something I picked up from the astral. Anyway, I learned that affection is a basic human need. You shouldn't let anything get in the way of expressing Love. Maybe it's even more basic than that... just hug someone.

Exploring

December 14, 2021

Last night I felt like APing after a few days of just going to sleep. I lay down and spent a few moments programming myself for an exit. Then I let go and fell asleep. After a few minutes I went into a trance and found myself floating out of my body and lucid.

I headed out of my room and went outside. My astral Mom was outside looking at the stars. I was a little surprised to find her in my AP. When this happens I usually ignore her because I cannot be totally sure she's my Mom or a dream entity. It just makes me uncomfortable for some reason. I lifted off into the night sky leaving my Mom behind and flew down the street.

I decided to check out the "party house" first. It's this house at the end of the street where I can usually find some girls to party with. I usually find something going on in there. I saw that the lights were on so I landed and headed in. It was deserted and it did not look as usual. Someone had changed the decor. I found a long hallway with lots of doors. Outside one door was a pink light so I went in. Inside I found a cute girl waiting for me. I introduced myself and she was super friendly and we ended up kissing for a while but not much more. I left and exited the house.

I ended up exploring much more. I found myself in a park with a large pool in the center. I had been lucid for so long I got a little worried about my physical body for some reason. I knew if I dove into the water the shock would probably wake me. So that's what I did... I dove into the water and woke up back at home.

I have a lot of these types of APs... where I exit and just explore. I try posting the most interesting APs/dreams but it's always a pleasure to get out of body and just go exploring! There is so much to see and things in the astral have a special look to them like if you were seeing with extra sensory vision. I also try to keep my eyes open for any special people I might want to meet. Astral people can also be very interesting!

Crowd

December 26, 2021

I exited but I was in my old house - the one I had grown up in when I was a teenager. I slept in the basement in my own room. Well, after I climbed out of my bed I felt wonderful - like really being Home. That's when I heard a scream from a woman outside my room. I went out of the room and saw that 3 people were in my basement and they were watching television. It looked like a horror movie. At this point I don't think my discriminating mind was working fully because I got mad and confronted the 3 people. "What are you doing in my house? Get out or I'll call the police!"

I looked around and there were like 10 more people in the room. They put on the stereo and where dancing and making so much noise. I got on the phone and called the police. They arrived and kicked everyone out of my house. The last thing I remember was going back to sleep in my cozy bed in the basement. That Home feeling had returned. Ahh...

City of Light

December 27, 2021

Then last night I exited in my current house and went outside. It was nighttime and there where long cirrus clouds in a starry sky. I flew up high in the air and headed east toward the coast. I flew over a big hill but instead of the open sea there was a huge lit city with beautiful skyscrapers and bridges and sparkly waterways that reflected all the lights.

I was awestruck at the beauty of this city and I remembered that I have been here a few times. There's some places in the astral that I keep visiting. I've been in this city like three times now. I flew down where the movie theater was, landed, and went inside. It's a magnificent theater and it looked very familiar. I went into one of the movies and stood in the back for a while to see what they were playing. All I remember is seeing an image of a couple drinking aqua-blue wine on a high terrace apartment over the city. The guy was wiping away the girl's tears with a light green handkerchief and she was smiling. He was saying, "Everything is going to be ok." That's all I saw...

I headed out of the movie and climbed some stairs and then went out a window. I flew but I was so high. I could see the city below and the sun was rising and I could see a bridge. The colors of the sky where so vivid and I got paranoid because I was so high up in the sky. The sun was half out of the water and it looked like an orange orb. It was breathtaking. I straightened out and just flew.

Running from the Mob

January 2, 2022

I went to sleep and tranced myself and was soon able to slip out of body. It wasn't my ordinary room but my room at my father's farm. I was alone - for now. I saw that my computer was hooked up on my desk and I went over to it to play with it. I work on a video game in real life and it was all there but in living color. I played on my computer for a while until I heard someone say, "What you working on?" I jumped. I looked over and there were three people in the room staring at me. I totally felt weirded out and left the room. They followed me.

I ran out toward the orange groves and as I looked back there where 20 people running after me. A girl was screaming something at me that I didn't understand. In front of me appeared a wall of glass and there was a door. I went through the glass and found a second door. This door was wooden and it wasn't attached to any walls. It was just sitting there in space. I opened it and went in.

As soon as I was on the other side I closed the door. I looked about and I was inside a small house. It looked homey and I felt safer. I looked around and it had a nice bed and entertainment system with a beanbag just like at home. I looked outside the window and it was a beautiful spring day. It looked like I was in a nice neighborhood because I saw a backyard and a house beyond.

I fell into the beanbag and turned on the television to see what astral tv would look like. Some cool sci-fi show started playing and I started really dreaming... I don't remember much after that except I felt like I was home.

Nighttime Purrs

January 16, 2022

So last night I AP and as I get off the bed I see something run after me! Apparently there was a cat on the bed with me. I looked down and there is my dead cat Indy from 20 years ago! I started petting him and he instantly started purring. I was so happy to see him and to know that he had been protecting my sleep without me knowing all this time. It really was him... I woke up and I was so happy I had little tears going. Awww... my kitty.

Astral Apps

January 23, 2022

I became lucid inside a new home I'd never been in. I was especially lucid and had full access to my astral self. You know, that special being with astral knowledge. I found my room and immediately got to work on my app. I sat down at my desk and there were two tablets there. Somehow I could input astral thoughts into them. I knew what I was doing and it was fascinating. It was like inputting code into a computer but the screens remained blank. Yet, I was working at lightning speed with a vast experience of knowledge in creating astral programs.

I finished my astral app and got ready for the party where I would unveil it to the community. I called up my friend and we headed to the astral showers to get ready for our big date. When we got there I realized that the astral showers where like another app. It had been created by a similar process as to what I had been doing. Me and my friend went up to the scanner and it scanned us and then recommended the proper shampoo and soap. There was a guy there taking care of the shower app. He kept tying to read my thoughts but was pretty much a nice guy.

After we were clean we headed out to the party where I would unveil my app. We arrived at this place that looked like a dance hall. Mostly everyone there was a girl. We set up and the first girls made a line to be the first to use my app. I gave my tablet to the girl and asked her to imagine the feeling of being on the perfect date. In a few seconds a beautiful dress replaced her clothes. She was so happy to have her perfect dress. So that's what my app did… it scanned her and made the perfect dress for her to wear on a date.

Many girls came up and used my app and I was congratulated on a great job. People were making copies of the app on their tablets or these little eggs people had. One girl came up to me and asked me if I wanted to go on a date with her. She had on one of my stunning dresses. I said yes and we left for a night on the town.

It was an interesting AP… but what interested me the most was that I had these skills to create astral apps. I knew exactly what I was doing and it really made me happy while I was creating. I think the astral is full of these astral apps. There are schools for them even to learn how to make astral apps. Maybe on some planes creating astral apps is a cool thing and kind of important to the functioning of reality.

Durabones

January 25, 2022

I was falling asleep and felt like it was enough so I attempted a separation. I had to force it a little but I detached, fell out of bed, and found myself on the floor. It's very important you don't flip out or rush at this point or you'll wake up. So I gently got off the floor (which was awkward) and was finally able to make it outside.

As I open the door I realize my astral Mom is calling me. She must of heard the door open. "Is that you honey? Where are you going?" I say, "I am going out - I'm APing! Come and look!" I go outside to the driveway and in a few moments see her come to the door. "Watch this Mom!" And I lift myself off the floor and start flying down the street. "I'll be back soon! Cya!"

The night was dark but some houses had lights on. I choose one with their lights on, land, and go inside. I see a man there but I think he can't see me. He's watching football and I think he's dreaming. His son walks though the door and they start talking. I still think they can't see me so I check out the rest of the house. In one room upstairs is a cute blond girl on her bed. She's reading a book on her back. I don't want to wake her up so I gently gently kiss her. She finally notices me and we start kissing in vigor. She seems kind of sad so we talk about some of her problems. Then she turns into a little cat and buries herself in the blanket. I go downstairs and exit the house. The man and son are still watching football.

I lift into the sky and notice there's a little more light in the sky. I go across the street which is suddenly this weird compound and meet this African family. I talk to the daughter awhile and then she tells me her Dad wants me to leave so I do. I ask her where they are from, and she says Zimbabwe. Wow.

I make it back to my neighborhood and it's looking like a beautiful sky blue fall day. The trees are all kinds of color. I go way up high, and can see all my haunts. I see that Durabones is on her hammock so I go to say hi. She's this cute blond that lives in my astral neighborhood. Sometimes she's on this hammock by a field and sometimes she brings friends there.

We greet like old friends and start talking about all kinds of things. Soon one of her boyfriends joins us and we start showing each other pictures from our lives. She's in high school and she shows me pics of herself at the school. We went on like that for like 30 minutes. A girlfriend of her joins us after that. Then we made three-wheeled motorcycles and a buggy. Durabones and her girlfriend got in the buggy and we hitched it up to a motorcycle. I got on the cycle and the other boy got on his and we just rode! I woke up right after that.

Blue Spheres

February 2, 2021

This was an unusual AP because it took place in a state I am unfamiliar with. I became lucid inside some kind of sphere. There was blue light everywhere and there was someone there with me. I don't exactly remember his words just that he was there to help me on this journey. The person pointed toward the center of the sphere where there was another sphere in blue light. We went deeper and deeper into the sphere finding smaller and smaller spheres as we got closer to the center.

I don't know how many spheres we crossed but me and my guide made it into the very center. There was final sphere here about the size of my fist. My guide said to grab the sphere and hold on as long as I could.

I took the small sphere in both hands and at first it was awkward - it kept trying to slide out from my grip. The more I stopped trying to fight it the more control I got. Finally I was able to hold unto the sphere of light but only for a few moments. It overwhelmed me with awareness - a special kind of awareness. It was like I was at the center of my very being. The more I played with the center sphere I realized that the only reason it resisted me was because I had some internal hangups about accepting who I was. The more I accepted the more the sphere and me melded together.

I remember at the end I accepted myself fully and the sphere went into my heart. I wonder who that guide was... he seemed faceless only like a silhouette.

Astral Mega-City

February 13, 2022

I went lucid sometime during the night. The next thing I know is that I am driving down a dark country road in my old car from high-school, one of my first cars, a white crown victoria. Somehow I am in the midst of a thinking process... I know that my ex=girlfriend is coming down the sidewalk in a bicycle in about 5 minutes. I pull over under a tree and there are shadows of the moon on the ground. I smoke a cigarette and lean on my car as I wait for my girl to appear.

Then I see her coming up the sidewalk in a white and pink bicycle. She is startled at first by the surprise. We talk and at first she's reluctant but eventually gets in my car. We go to the city and have some fun eventually ending up on a talk show about freedom and the problems depending on systems. We argued that if it could all be lived in the moment there wouldn't be a need for depending on systems. Some of the judges argued we needed systems while some said life could be lived in the moment. Someone said we were just describing the mandala principle with one side being enlightenment and the other ignorance. "Ying-yang!" someone screamed.

Then we drifted from each other (me and my girlfriend) and she went her ways and I went mine. The last time I saw her she had hooked up with a guy who was rubbing her feet. I gave up on her after that and went my way.

I remember leaving the city, a mega astral city, after exploring it awhile. People just sort of would loose themselves going from one dream to another commingling with each other and giving each other pleasure of some sort. I couldn't do it for long, it was almost like a trance. I left and headed for the highlands.

Am I a Ghost?

February 21, 2022

I've been exploring the nature of my astral world by exploring my neighborhood. Last night for example I APed and went across the street. The door was open and so I went inside. Inside are three kids hanging out in the livingroom. They were chatting amongst themselves. I wanted to test if they could see me so I moved in front of them. I waved my hands in front of them and theg acted like they couldn't see me.

Does this mean when I AP I am like a ghost? Are these people in the astral dreaming or are they people in the real world who are awake and I am accessing the real world like a phantasm?

I went up the stairs and found a woman laying on her bed talking to her husband. I walked into the room and they had no clue I was there. I sat down on the side of their bed and listened in on their conversation. It seemed like ordinary chit chat from their day.

I wondered what was in the rest of the house so I went into the last two rooms. A pretty girl was in one of them laying down on her bed. She was writing something. She didn't seem to notice me so I went up to her and kissed her on the mouth. As usual when I do this they sort of "wake up" and can see me for the first time. She started kissing back which is a typical reaction when I do this.

I still have many questions about these astral characters. Who are they? The people I saw aren't the ones that live in that house in the real world. And why can't they see me until I touch them? And why are they so easy to make them kiss me back? Maybe they are dreaming.

I also remember another AP where I went to one of these girls and asked if she could see me. She did not respond until I kissed her and then she said "of course I can see you." So maybe they can see me and are just choosing to ignore me. Why would they ignore me?

Many questions have I... the astral is a weird place. At least my neighborhood is.

Enlightened Earth

February 28, 2022

I had this dream a few nights ago and it's stuck with me. The dream was like a story... some kind of drama. Apparently, the Governments of the Higher Planes had decided that the Earth was spiritually ready to appoint an official Earth astral government or representation. This would be Earth's official presence on the Higher Planes.

The first thing to do was to broadcast the Intention. This was the call for all of the spiritually enlightened people on Earth to come together and form the first astral government.

The response was overwhelming! There were so many spiritually enlightened people on Earth and they all came together to form the first astral government. It was an amazing sight to see! They all had different backgrounds and beliefs, but they all came together for the common good.

They worked tirelessly to create a fair and just astral society that would benefit all of humanity. They were determined to make a difference in this world.

But then something happened... it was almost like the existence of the astral government polarized positive energies vs negative energies. They realized all the Negative Karma they still had.

The astral government was a beacon of light in a world full of darkness. It was a symbol of hope and change. And that's what the negative energies didn't like. They were threatened by the astral government and all that it stood for.

So, the negatives did what they do best... they started to spread lies and misinformation about the astral government. They tried to discredit it and turn the people against it saying astral Life was dark magic and witchcraft.

But the astral government was strong. It withstood the attacks and continued to serve the people. And the people continued to support it. They knew that the astral government was for the good of all.

Eventually, the negative energies gave up. They realized that they couldn't defeat the astral government. It was too strong and too loved by the people. Because it was helping All people. More and more people were Turning On and becoming Enlightened!

The astral government stood strong from that day, serving the people and making a difference in the world. Earth was welcomed as a proponent of the Higher Planes and massive enlightened and positive energies began to flow. Eventually Earth ascended into the higher cosmos...

Some Negative APs

March 16, 2022

A few nights ago I exited spontaneously. I get out of my body and go outside. Outside are like 5 guys waiting for me. When I tried to avoid them and move past them they get in my way and start pushing me around. To them it's all a big mean joke but underneath that I can tell these guys are really mad at me and really hate me. They force me into a big car and I'm like their hostage! In the car I try to talk to them and ask them what exactly I did. "You know what you did!" says one of the punks. They drive me out into the dark and the car stops and we all get out. They form a circle around me and that's when I decide to bolt.

I start running and suddenly there is this river in front of me. I dive in and start swimming across. The waters are dark and murky. I see the punks yelling at me to come back. I make it to the other side of the river and climb out. I start walking, more like running, since I feel like they may be coming after me. Eventually I wake up and I'm so glad to be safe at home.

Then I had this dream last night of this person in my house. I can tell he's negative and at one point he takes out his phone and shows me pictures of myself while I'm sleeping or supposed to be alone like he's been spying on me. That freaked me out. Then he shows me pictures of me with all my limbs twisted and broken. He laughs this evil little laugh and I jolt awake.

It's not all bad news though. A few nights ago I had a spectacular dream where I was in one of my fantasy stories I wrote when I was in college. It was so spectacular and real and colorful and vivid. It was so good that I wonder if it came from my imagination or if it was Heaven sent. What it really felt like was like as if a group of angels where using my story to cheer me up. Whoever these characters where they were in my corner and all of us participated in pushing the negative energy away. It reminded me why I do this... dreams like that are the epitomes of dreaming.

Too bad they don't happen more often.

Astral Alcohol

March 30, 2022

I had a successful exit last night and lifted out of my beanbag a little awkwardly. Sometimes it's tough getting out of my beanbag. It's like getting out of a large ball of cotton. So I go out my room and into the night. I go across the street and go inside a house with a light on. The ones with lights are always open and inviting. I explore the house and it's empty. The lights are on in every room.

In the master bedroom is a standing mirror and when I looked at my reflection it looked like I was 18. Somehow the mirror had depth so I push against it and it turns into a tunnel. I go inside. It leads straight and upwards. The walls where like a white cave, smooth and bumpy.

I exit into a starry night. There are hills and a river meandering through it. There is a small town below so I make my way to it. It takes me about 20 seconds to get to the town with this speed trick I know. You sort of do your floating and then put one hand directed forward and one hand directed backwards. And then you sort of pull air with your forward hand and expulse with your backward hand. Almost like a jet. I was there in seconds.

I go into town and there are neon signs everywhere. What look like bars and brothels are on each side of a generous street. I go into a pretty building with blue and pink neon. Inside I see cubicles with one person a piece. They are just standing there in their cubicle. So I go up to one person and ask what they are doing.

The guy asks me if I could use a friend for an hour or two. He quotes me some kind of price. I gather this is some kind of brothel. I exit the building and go down the street trying to read the signs. But they are in a very weird language I have never seen.

I go into what looks like a bar and it's very well lighted. The bartender asks me if I want to try their moonshine. He brings me a glass half-full of clear moonshine. It tastes like bitter water but goes down smoothly. And then I feel it. Astral alcohol!

I "went to sleep" soon after that and had pretty dreams. I was completely lucid for this one until the last part where I drifted away.

Star Children

April 7, 2022

Last night I had a story dream... one of those long visions that sometimes come during sleep. It was about a huge city filled with star children. The only thing was that this city was inside a huge spaceship. And inside were skyscrapers and houses and parks. There where so many star children that it was becoming uncomfortable to live in the spaceship - because there was no way out.

Somehow though two star children escaped and made it out of the city. They were so happy they were free. They journeyed throughout the astral and finally came to a world rich with Life. They found fertile forests where they could hide. Then one day a young man was exploring the woods when they chanced upon him. He was spending the night all by himself in the deep dark woods.

The star children approached him and read his thoughts. They felt the loneliness that he was feeling. That's when they came out from their hiding spot and sang to him. They turned into little lights that danced around him and sung him tales of the Universe. The boy was so happy that he accepted them into his Spirit and they became a Trio from that day on.

They had many adventures and learned many things from each other. Some other humans somehow noticed something special about this boy and started wondering about him. Some even began harassing him. The boy and the star children fought the bullies and gained much merit because of this. In time these three souls became legendary in some worlds and would be sent into messed up worlds to fix and balance their Spirit. They had so much merit that things could only get better for everyone.

To this day they travel together friends forever casting Light where the shadows encroach.

Astral Music

April 17, 2022

I became lucid in a crowd of people... we were on this grassy hill. One guy was mentioning to his friends to follow him. "Come see my new project," he was saying.

So we all followed him and suddenly there was amazing music playing. You could also see the music as a wave pattern and it was rippling in pink sending waves and waves into outer space. It was really beautiful. After the show everyone went their separate way. I caught up to one of the people who had been watching and said something like, "I wonder how one makes music do that?" The guy looked at me and that's when he turned toward me inquisitively. He takes out this gadget and says, "Stand still."

He scans my head with this gadget and says, "A few accomplishments, one big one..." He scans my right leg, "A slave to power..." He scans my left leg, "But also a healthy dose of freedom. Later dude." And he disappears over the hill.

Then the dream changed and I was in my old room at my father's farm. However, there was someone sitting on the bed - a nun in garb. It's interesting because we sold that farm to a covenant of nuns. The last time I heard about my father's farm, it had been taken over by nuns as a retreat. So when I saw that nun on my bed it kind of freaked me out. Am I haunting my old room at the farm? I have a lot of dreams about my Dad and he's always at the farm and now it's a retreat for nuns...

Ash Town/Color Town

April 23, 2022

I had a good exit last night. I just sort of floated vertically and then naturally assumed a standing position. It was kind of confusing because everything felt like normal waking reality. I wasn't 100% sure I had exited so I went into my bathroom and tried the light switch. It was non-operational. I tried to fly or float by using my hand jets and sure enough I lifted a few inches off the ground - I was asleep!

I went outside and it was pitch dark as sometimes happens. The houses had no lights on them. I went right and lifted into the air hunting for something interesting. As the road bent west that's when everything changed and I entered the wastelands. There was light coming from everywhere and everything was lighted in grays and whites. The buildings were this ash color like they had been burned but still maintained their shape. It was so quiet.

I wandered around and everything looked old and deserted. I remember being somewhere like this before. Ash Town. There was litter on the ground but it was ancient. I passed a wind mill, a skeleton of a tree, old mansions with dark windows, an old theater with a few letters on it. There seemed to be like a few locations but they melted together to form chaos... yet there was a beauty to it. Like an old forgotten astral environment where everything and everyone had moved on.

I went back the way I had come hoping to exit the town of ash. I found my street and flew back toward my neighborhood. When things started looking like normal I relaxed. I noticed my house and that I had left the door open. I went passed it and then Color Town appeared. It was day time and the houses looked like they were made of candy. They were so bright and colorful. The lawns looked perfectly manicured and all that bright green. There were no cars whatsoever - not one. I looked at the houses and the windows where the only dark areas.

Something spooked me about this neighborhood. It was just too perfect and new. The sky was blue, blue, blue without one cloud marking it. I decided to go back to my house before getting lost. And I really didn't want to go into any houses this time. But it was a gorgeous neighborhood - just kind of creepy that desolation.

I found my house after some back flying and landed in my driveway. I went in and closed the door and went in my room and lay down and fell asleep.

Bricks

May 5, 2022

I think I was having a dream when something happened and my awareness became instantly clear and lucid. It was like a part of me needed help so the whole of me arrived. The first thing I know is that four bullies are surrounding this small little teen of a girl. They are taunting her and she's about to cry. My first reaction lucidly is to kick some butt. So I barrel into the group, do some yelling and pushing, and the bullies flee. I acquaint myself with the girl and we become friends. She says she wants to take me Home to meet her family. She's so sweet and cute, thin, with blond short hair. She holds my hand and reality sort of folds in on itself and we're suddenly in another place.

It's beautiful with lots of trees on one side and a great dirt plain on the other. I look at this dirt plain but it's not really dirt. The ground is made of little bricks all the way to the horizon. I inspect one of the bricks and it's made of even smaller rectangles like cells.

She takes me to her house which is made of bricks too. There are nice plants on and around the small house. I meet her Mom and Dad and her little sister. They are super nice and we hang out in the kitchen for a while. Then she says if I'd like to go to the Border to help the shiblings. (I don't exactly know what a shibling is.) I agree to go with her and she packs a picnic basket and we walk to the border on this brick road.

When we get there I see what a shibling is. They are the people who make the bricks. They make the astral world bigger and bigger. I see tons of newly made bricks on the ground. They look like they are drying or being prepared. Everything is kind of dark and brown though. But the bricks are very pretty almost like the road, amber and honey colored.

We stayed with the shiblings and shared the food. I remember giving her a hug goodbye and saying something like, "I'm about to wake up! I have to go!" and then I was back in my bed.

Two Wolves

May 12, 2022

I was driving in this realistic dream and when I looked over my girlfriend was on the other side of the car next to me. I was driving my old crown vic for some reason and it was white. My girlfriend said to pull over into a dirt road and in a few minutes a big old white mansion appeared. It looked a little dilapidated but I had been here before. It's really a school for spiritual endeavors. It seems to be one of my astral girlfriend's favorite places to visit in dream land.

We went to the back porch after greeting everyone. We lay in this cushion thing that overlooked the lake. I planted a hundred kisses on her face and she smiled and laughed. Then we went inside to the library.

We started watching a film. As we watched this film what was happening in the film tangled together with our dreams. First there was a dark wolf that crossed a rope bridge. That wolf was me. Then a white wolf appeared that was my girlfriend and she hesitated at the bridge. Then the white wolf started going out of shape like her profile was drawn in angled lines. But then a light brown wolf appeared and helped the white wolf. Finally, she started looking like normal and crossed the bridge to me.

As the two wolfs got together on the other side I feel someone grab me in a huge hug and laugh into the crook of my neck. I hugged her back and there were more happy kisses.

Mahayana

May 19, 2022

I was trying to exit, and I was in that half-between state, when the background turns white and I see the cartoon outline of this Wonder Woman girl appear. She was being redrawn like 10 times a second until it produced this animated layering effect. She had a crown of yellow, then blue, then violet, all kinds of colors. And she seemed drawn with a super hero uniform. After that came two more super women, also drawn on a bright background of white.

They started speaking to me and said this: "This is the Mahayana…" A thousand petaled white lotus appeared this time in 3D. It twirled and began unfolding. "It leads to this…" Now an 8 petaled pink lotus appeared. I think the 8 represent the 8 virtues of Buddhism or the Noble 8 Fold Path.

After that I became lucid in this huge carpeted room. It was empty except for me laying down in my bean-bag (which was also there) and this huge wooden whale. From my bean-bag I checked out this whale. It was carved with all kinds of designs and strange languages. I see this woman with short hair appear so I get up and go and talk to her.

"Where'd you come from?" she asks.

I say something like, "I'm looking for someone that can teach me the full Mahayana."

"Ahh… the Mahayana. I know it well. What's with the whale?"

"I think it belonged to my former Master."

"That's interesting. Look in the mirror." I looked into one of the mirrors on the wall and I had a big bruise on the left side of my face.

"Don't worry... I'll watch out for you. I take care of a lot of people," she says.

We went into a kitchen where a few people where making a meal. She handed me a small knife and said, "Cut these carrots."

And that's all I remember. I looked up the Mahayana today and went over a few of my books on it. Kind of inspires me to seek some formal training.

Another Life

May 28, 2022

Last night I had a lucid experience that's worth writing down. I went to sleep and woke up in another world. I was still me but I lived downtown in a beautiful city. Everything was modern and the buildings were futuristic. I was lucid but as this other me. I did my morning routine and then headed off to work. Apparently I worked at this astral company that made astral apps.

I walked into work which was called Stormfront Studios and I knew everyone there. It was like I had been given access to many more memories of mine and I knew everyone's names. It was more than that... I was actually familiar with all of them. I went into my office and worked on the app. It was an app designed to replace an older environment with new material... I think. I had a computer and some kind of terminal I could input and read data from.

I talked to many people and engaged in several meetings with these new people which were very familiar with me and which I counted as old friends.

I left work and got ready for my third date with this girl I had been seeing. Tonight I was planning to kiss her for the first time. We met and it was a great date. I walked her home and at her door I kissed her. She was shy at first but then she fell in with me and we kissed for real.

Light Filaments

June 1, 2022

This one was kind of odd but in a good way. I had a dream of some kind of different reality. I didn't have a body, I was just awareness.

It consisted of great tubes that led to these collections of intricate light filaments. I would visit one center of light filaments and then I would take a tube at top speed to another center of filaments. I did this for a while and they all had different colors, and shapes, and patterns of lighting up.

I would connect to the center of filaments and I would sort of commune with it and make myself part of it. It felt like I was flipping switches deep inside these centers. As soon as I was done I would rush through the tubes to another center.

I was thinking maybe this was my unconscious mind doing some healing... or just operating inside my body or mind?

Conclusion

Thank you for reading all my crazy astral projections! If it's one thing I've learned from all my adventures is that the Universe is full of surprises. Just as I think nothing could top one of my latest APs another one comes along that makes me rethink everything. If we can learn to astral project we are embarking on a fantastic journey – a journey that will fill us with wonder and change us forever.

I did not want to speculate too much on exiting techniques because I believe that once you are ready to astral project it will happen naturally. You will develop your own exiting techniques. What works for some people will not always work for someone else. What I recommend however, is that you always strive for the Light. It will quicken your way to the worlds beyond and guarantee your journey toward becoming a free astral being. Striving toward the Light does not particularly mean becoming austere or repentant. It just means that you cause as little suffering as possible and always try to be a good person. It's that easy. Slowly but surely, you'll cross all those thresholds that lead upwards into the Cosmos.

With fond wishes I wish you joyous astral projections and Godspeed to the worlds beyond!

Made in the USA
Middletown, DE
06 September 2022

73376859R00096